Much Ado about Nothing

Edited by

Roma Gill, OBE
M.A. *Cantab.*, B. Litt. *Oxon*

D1719476

OXFORD
UNIVERSITY PRESS

OXFORD
UNIVERSITY PRESS

Great Clarendon Street, Oxford OX2 6DP

Oxford University Press is a department of the University of Oxford.
It furthers the University's objective of excellence in research,
scholarship, and education by publishing worldwide in

Oxford   New York

Auckland   Cape Town   Dar es Salaam   Hong Kong   Karachi
Kuala Lumpur   Madrid   Melbourne   Mexico City   Nairobi
New Delhi   Shanghai   Taipei   Toronto

With offices in

Argentina   Austria   Brazil   Chile   Czech Republic   France   Greece
Guatemala   Hungary   Italy   Japan   Poland   Portugal   Singapore
South Korea   Switzerland   Thailand   Turkey   Ukraine   Vietnam

Oxford is a registered trade mark of Oxford University Press
in the UK and in certain other countries

British Library Cataloguing in Publication

Data available

ISBN 978 0 19 832872 8

10 9 8 7

Printed in Great Britain by Bell and Bain Ltd., Glasgow.

The Publisher would like to thank the
following for permission to reproduce
photographs:

Ronald Grant Archive: pp. v; xxii

Cover artwork by Silke Bachmann
Illustrations by Alexy Pendle

For Katy

Oxford School Shakespeare
edited by Roma Gill
with additional material by Judith Kneen

Macbeth
Much Ado About Nothing
Henry V
Romeo & Juliet
A Midsummer Night's Dream
Twelfth Night
Hamlet
The Merchant of Venice
Othello
Julius Caesar
The Tempest
The Taming of the Shrew
King Lear
As You Like It
Antony and Cleopatra
Measure for Measure
Henry IV Part I
The Winter's Tale
Coriolanus
Love's Labour's Lost
Richard II

Contents

Introduction

About the Play

Have you ever been in love – or do you hope one day to fall in love? Answer 'Yes' (privately) to one of these questions, and you can read *Much Ado About Nothing* with sympathy. Answer 'No', and you can laugh to see how easily others can be beguiled. (But beware! You may not escape all that easily.)

Shakespeare's imagination knew love in all its moods – from its first surprised awakening to its final hopeless despair, from the comedy of love discovered to the tragedy of love lost for ever. No one knew better than he that 'The course of true love never did run smooth'[1]. Love is a major theme – often the only theme – in more than twenty of his plays, in both his narrative poems, and in almost all of his 154 sonnets.

In many of his comedies, Shakespeare develops and contrasts the love affairs of two young women. One of them is usually described as small and dark, the other tall and fair. Their respective

partners are usually far less interesting than the women themselves. For each play the action is basically the same: a love is declared, is challenged, and is finally reasserted in the harmony of marriage. Although the titles of the plays may suggest that their subjects are unimportant (Such as *As You Like It*, *Twelfth Night – or What You Will*), the poetry communicates intense emotions and shows Shakespeare to be fully engaged with his characters, and deeply concerned about them.

The title of *Much Ado About Nothing*, apparently making a pun on 'nothing' and 'noting' (two words which had the same pronunciation in Shakespeare's

---

[1] *A Midsummer Night's Dream*, Act 1, Scene i, line 134.

day), seems to question its own seriousness. 'Nothing'? Is it nothing that 'Men were deceivers ever' (Act II, Scene iii, line 63)? Slander and misrepresentation are among Shakespeare's greatest evils, for which there can be no forgiveness and which, in *Othello*, will give rise to one of his greatest tragedies. *Much Ado* foreshadows this, anticipating the darker humour which will dominate the next phase of Shakespeare's writing in such plays as *Measure for Measure* and *All's Well That Ends Well*.

For *Much Ado*, however, the end of the play is laughter and dancing. Hero's near-tragedy is avoided and the wit and delight of Beatrice and Benedick take centre stage, as they have done ever since the seventeenth century:

> . . . let but Beatrice
> And Benedick be seen, lo in a trice
> The Cockpit, galleries, boxes, are all full . . .
>
> Leonard Digges
> (1640; prefatory poem for Shakespeare's *Poems*)

Leading Characters in the Play

Don Pedro The Prince of Aragon. He has won a victory over his illegitimate brother, and is visiting Messina on his way home.

Don John The illegitimate brother of Don Pedro. A stage direction describes him as 'the Bastard', and he describes himself as 'a plain-dealing villain'.

Claudio A young nobleman who has has been honoured for his conduct in the recent fighting, but is still very immature and naive in his judgements.

Benedick A follower of Don Pedro. His name (*benedictus*) means 'the blessed one'. He has adopted a pose of woman-hater, and swears he will never marry.

Borachio A follower and friend of Don John, and the originator of the scheme to discredit Hero. His name comes from the Spanish word for 'wine-bottle'.

Leonato The Governor of Messina and father of Hero. He is flattered by the attentions of Don Pedro, and quick to believe whatever the prince tells him.

Hero The daughter of Leonato, described by Claudio as 'a modest young lady', and dismissed by Benedick as 'too low for a high praise, and too little for a great praise'. Her name may have been suggested by *Hero and Leander*, a narrative poem (published 1598) by Christopher Marlowe, which tells of the tragedy of two lovers in Greek mythology.

Beatrice Although Leonato is 'her uncle and her guardian', the position of Beatrice in Leonato's family and household is unclear. She speaks and behaves with more than usual freedom, and her witty intelligence presents a challenge to all the male characters. Her name, like that of Benedick, means 'the blessed one' (*beatrix*), and she too has sworn never to marry.

Dogberry Master Constable of Messina. He has a great opinion of himself and his office but has an imperfect mastery of the English language. Shakespeare may have designed the role for Will Kemp, a famous and accomplished actor of low-comedy roles.

Verges Headborough (under-constable), Dogberry's assistant. The role may have been designed for Richard Cowley, another comic actor whose pale complexion and scrawny limbs, contrasting with the burly physique of Will Kemp, may have suggested the character's name – 'verjuice' was the vinegary, acid juice of unripe fruit, used in medicine and cooking.

Synopsis

Act 1

SCENE 1 Leonato welcomes Don Pedro to his house. Beatrice and Benedick are quarrelling, but Claudio speaks of his love for Hero.

SCENE 2 Leonato is told a false rumour about Don Pedro's intentions towards Hero.

SCENE 3 Don John plans mischief.

Act 2

SCENE 1 A masked ball: Don Pedro talks of love; Benedick is teased by Beatrice; Claudio is misled (but the mistake is corrected); and Hero is betrothed to Claudio. Don Pedro makes another plan: to bring Benedick and Beatrice together.

SCENE 2 Borachio pleases Don John with his new scheme to discredit Hero.

SCENE 3 Benedick is tricked into believing that Beatrice loves him.

Act 3

SCENE 1 Beatrice is tricked into believing that Benedick loves her.

SCENE 2 Don Pedro and Claudio are both deceived by Don John's slander of Hero.

SCENE 3 The Watchmen make an arrest.

SCENE 4 Hero is preparing for her wedding.

SCENE 5 Leonato is too busy to listen to Dogberry's report on the arrest.

ACT 4

ACT 5

Much Ado About Nothing: Commentary

ACT I

SCENE I The happy opening of the scene establishes an atmosphere which will continue (though not unbroken) throughout the play. An easy, relaxed prose is used to show this is a civilized society, courtly in manners, but free from the court's formality (as suggested in the affected speech of the messenger). It is always ready to burst from wit to laughter.

Leonato, the governor of Messina, is delighted to welcome and entertain the Prince of Aragon. Hero and Beatrice, Leonato's daughter and niece, look forward to receiving the prince's followers. In appearance and temperament the two young women are very different: dark-haired Hero, small and quiet, contrasts with the vivacious Beatrice, tall and fair. Beatrice is eager for news, interrupting the elaborate courtesies of the messenger and deliberately mistaking his careful speeches until the poor man, bewildered by such unladylike behaviour, is rescued by Hero and Leonato, who are listening in amusement. Their conversation allows time for the prince's party to catch up with their herald and appear on the stage.

Already the audience knows enough to identify the different characters: Don Pedro, Prince of Aragon, victorious from a recent battle; a young officer called Claudio who has behaved with distinction in the fighting; and the object of Beatrice's interest, 'Signor Montanto' – otherwise known as 'Signor Benedick of Padua' – who engages immediately with her in a quickfire exchange of insults. Both are determined to remain single, professing themselves haters of marriage and making it clear that they have no attachments: 'truly I love none' says Benedick, and Beatrice is quick to agree – 'I thank God and my cold blood I am of your humour'.

Also in the prince's entourage is a man who, amidst the general warmth of greeting, stands cold and aloof: Don John. A shadow seems to pass over the company with his abrupt acknowledgement of Leonato's hospitality, but this is dispersed when Leonato and Don Pedro lead the way into the house.

Claudio, however, detains Benedick with man-to-man confidences concerning Leonato's daughter, a 'modest young lady'. He has conceived a most poetic passion for her which is not to be quenched by the cold water of Benedick's scorn. Marriage, to Benedick, means running the risk of becoming a cuckold – a husband of an unfaithful wife. This is a pitiful state for those involved, but a constant source of amusement for outsiders. The scepticism of Don Pedro, returning to seek his companions, provokes Benedick to further extravagant remarks against women – and the audience waits happily for the turn of events that will show us 'Benedick, the married man'.

Tactfully despatching Benedick on some (probably unnecessary) errand, Don Pedro can turn his attentions to Claudio, who speaks the first verse line of the play as the mood changes from everyday banter and friendly courtesy to serious discussion:

My liege, your highness now may do me good. (line 264)

Claudio's love seems to be diplomatic as well as passionate: his social status and his military career have both been taken into consideration before the 'soft and delicate desires' were allowed to prompt his present appeal for Don Pedro's help. Perhaps the conventions of his society require that such affairs are conducted through an intermediary – or perhaps Claudio is too shy to address Hero for himself! But Don Pedro agrees to be his spokesman and, disguised as Claudio in the social gathering promised for that same evening, he will declare his love and win Hero's heart.

The stage is set, the characters are prepared – and the audience can have little doubt about the final outcome. But the best laid plans often go astray . . .

SCENE 2 . . . and Don Pedro's words have been overheard and misunderstood. Leonato is told that he should make sure Hero is prepared to receive a *royal* proposal. This mistake was innocent enough – but there is worse to follow because . . .

SCENE 3 . . . another listener, with more accurate hearing, has heard Don Pedro and Claudio speaking of Hero. Now Borachio reports his intelligence to Don John, lifting him out of his depression so that he can begin to take the role he has identified for himself: 'I am a plain-dealing villain'. Evil, full-blooded melodramatic evil, has come into the happy world of Leonato's Messina. It is directed, with Don John's bitter, sardonic humour, at 'the most exquisite Claudio', the 'young start-up' who has 'all the glory of [Don John's] overthrow'. Gleefully meditating revenge, Don John the Bastard leads his informer into Leonato's 'great supper'.

ACT 2

SCENE 1   After their supper, the family reassembles. Beatrice is showing her sharp wit in a conversation with the old men where horns, the symbols of cuckoldry, are once again a main source of amusement. In this society, it seems, women as well as men assume that faithlessness is inevitable among married couples. Hero, however, is silent: she cannot share in the freedom that Beatrice enjoys through having no parents to frame her destiny. Hero knows that she must be 'ruled by [her] father' – and he, believing what Antonio told him, has prepared his daughter to receive a proposal from the prince himself.

The guests come together, and the evening's 'revelling' – a masked ball – begins. Such entertainments were popular with the Elizabethans, perhaps because the masks (which could be elaborate, or grotesque) gave more than usual freedom to those who joined in the fun. As each couple comes downstage, the audience, for a moment, overhears the different conversations. Don Pedro's meaning we can understand – but Hero's responses are cautious; Balthasar makes an approach to Margaret (who rejects him) and Ursula is cheeky to old Antonio; Beatrice, perhaps recognizing Benedick, takes the opportunity to taunt and even insult him – and his mask cannot cover the dismay and hurt that he feels.

Outside the dance and wearing no festive mask, Don John pretends to mistake the disguised Claudio for Benedick and tells him that Don Pedro is courting Hero for himself. Borachio is quick to give support to this story, and Claudio is even more convinced of his betrayal when Benedick (himself deceived by appearances) offers his sympathy. Like a boy thinking himself beaten by a man, Claudio surrenders his claims with no further argument: he lacks the strength and resources to fight back against a prince. Luckily he has a friend, and Benedick (despite his own hurt) takes up Claudio's cause, tactfully reproaching his prince for unfair behaviour. Don Pedro soon puts his mind at rest – and then listens to Benedick's own complaint as he explodes in semi-comic wrath against Beatrice.

Benedick has been stung to the quick, utterly demoralized, his manhood threatened – and he hides his embarrassment in a rapid escape when Beatrice approaches. Don Pedro remonstrates with her on Benedick's behalf. But the reproaches meet with careless dismissal from Beatrice, who hints at an earlier injustice that she had received from Benedick when he 'won [her heart] with false dice'.

Beatrice has brought with her the bruised Claudio, now sullen and submissive before the prince. Even after the mistake has been cleared up, he seems unable to speak for himself, and needs to be urged on by Beatrice to take Hero by the hand. Here the formal language of Claudio and Leonato is enough, with the token kiss that is given and received, to constitute a legally binding 'marriage by pre-contract':

Leonato
Count, take of me my daughter, and with her my
fortunes. His grace hath made the match, and all
grace say amen to it.

Claudio
Lady, as you are mine, I am yours.

This is a solemn moment but it is soon dissolved by Beatrice, who looks on the happy couple and compares her own single condition, although her words may not be altogether light-hearted. She easily turns away Don Pedro's (half-serious) offer, saying: 'Your grace is too costly to wear every day', and obeys her uncle's dismissal to household duties – 'will you look to those things I told you of?'

When Beatrice has left the room, Don Pedro voices the thought that must be in everyone's mind: 'She were an excellent wife for Benedick.' Once more Don Pedro will be a go-between – but this time for two reluctant lovers.

SCENE 2 This scene shows the beginnings of another plot – but how different in tone and intention! Don John's hatred has grown until he is 'sick in displeasure', and he will snatch at any suggestion to hurt Claudio. Borachio's idea is to make Claudio think that he is mocked, as well as betrayed, when he hears the supposed Hero call an unknown midnight lover by his name.

Don John may seem slow to understand Borachio's scheme, but it is important that the audience should know all the details: we shall never *see* the much-discussed rendezvous, and there is no time to ask awkward questions (just how is Borachio going to 'fashion the matter' so that Hero is not in her own chamber on the night before her wedding?) because we are quickly presented with . . .

SCENE 3 . . . another virtuoso performance from Benedick as he laments the change in Claudio and his own loss of a soldier-friend – lost to marriage while Benedick enjoys his bachelor freedom! But the prince and Claudio, with music and poetry, begin to lay their siege – using love's proper medium, verse, before changing back to prose for their plotting. At first their attempts are clumsy but, with a little nudging and urging, they manage to persuade Leonato, from his privileged position as Hero's father, to provide them with evidence of Beatrice's love: 'My daughter tells us all.' Overhearing praise for Beatrice and criticism of himself convinces Benedick to reconsider his position – 'When I said I would die a bachelor, I did not think I should live till I were married'.

When Beatrice comes reluctantly to call him to dinner, he slips somewhat awkwardly into the lover's role and thanks her with a regular verse line: 'Fair Beatrice, I thank you for your pains.'

Interpreting Beatrice's answers to suit his altered opinion of her, and encouraged by his own arguments, Benedick takes a positive step forward: 'I will go get her picture.'

ACT 3

SCENE 1 The second stage of Don Pedro's scheme runs smoothly from the very beginning. Hero, having made sure that Beatrice will overhear, takes evident delight in talking over her cousin's faults and failings with Ursula. The gentle Hero proves a sharp critic: Beatrice is 'so self-endear'd . . . so odd and from all fashions' that her conduct 'cannot be commendable', and Benedick, loving her not wisely but too well, should be advised 'to fight against his passion' and rather 'waste inwardly' than 'die with mocks'. Ursula, tongue in cheek, attempts to mitigate Hero's censure: Beatrice 'cannot be so much without true judgement' as to reject Signor Benedick, who is 'foremost in report through Italy'.

Beatrice, overhearing, is immediately struck with remorse and love – a love which expresses itself in what is almost a sonnet (two quatrains and a couplet). This verse deftly closes up the scene.

SCENE 2 Smartened up and newly shaven (perhaps he heard that Beatrice 'could not endure a husband with a beard on his face' – Act II, Scene i, line 25), Benedick takes Leonato away for 'eight or nine wise words' – much to the amusement of Don Pedro and Claudio. But the gloomy Don John, his malice disguised as duty and favour, breaks into their delight with strange hints, bemoaning the 'suit ill spent, and labour ill bestowed' that has linked Claudio with Hero – 'Leonato's Hero, your Hero, every man's Hero'. Each repetition of her name adds force to his accusations, and he describes the (artfully staged) scene they can witness at Hero's bedchamber window in such detail that his words alone are enough to convince his hearers of Hero's guilt. The scene ends in an operatic chorus of lamentation –

Don Pedro
O day untowardly turned!

Claudio
O mischief strangely thwarting!

Don John
O plague right well prevented!

But before the audience can worry unduly about the sudden alteration in Claudio, the mood of the play switches from high melodrama to low comedy.

SCENE 3   Dogberry, Master Constable, assembles the Watch for a briefing on the night's duties. His self-importance bursts through his speech in grand malapropisms – mistaken words that sometimes express the opposite of his intended meaning ('desertless' for 'deserving', 'tolerable' for 'intolerable'). The police force is made up of unpaid local citizens (they can avoid these duties by paying for a substitute), and their incompetence is an easy source of entertainment.

Borachio and Conrad are now overheard by the watchmen as they discuss Don John's scheme. Borachio, drunk with success, boasts of his performance in the charade that has deceived Claudio and Don Pedro. Conrad, bemused by talk of 'fashion' as a 'deformed thief' that can alter a man's appearance, is slow to understand, forcing Borachio to explain exactly what has happened – and what is going to happen the next morning when Claudio meets Hero for the wedding, 'as he was appointed'.

The Watch have heard enough, and in the arrest of Borachio and Conrad the audience knows that they have indeed 'recovered the most dangerous piece of lechery that ever was known in the commonwealth'.

SCENE 4   It is with heightened suspense that we watch Hero preparing for her wedding. She is understandably nervous and irritable, but oddly depressed – 'my heart is exceeding heavy' – and impatient with Margaret's bawdy jokes, which are further fuelled when Beatrice complains of feeling ill. Margaret immediately guesses the cause, and has fun with puns about *carduus benedictus* (the 'holy thistle' cure-all remedy).

SCENE 5   Elsewhere in the house Leonato is far too busy to listen to Dogberry's ramblings, and the 'examination' of the 'two auspicious persons' has to be delegated to the delighted Dogberry.

Act 4

SCENE 1   The wedding party assembles. Disaster, we know, must come soon, and the audience welcomes Leonato's request that Friar Francis 'be brief', but even so, Claudio's curt answer to the friar's question comes as a shock:

> **Friar**
> You come hither, my lord, to marry this lady?
> **Claudio**
> No.

The ceremonious opening quickly gives way to Claudio's anger. His accusations are bitter, and he spits out the word 'maid' with vicious repetition in the stinging verse lines. Claudio has (he feels) been deeply insulted, and the nervous under-current of unease that has bubbled through the play in jokes about cuckolds' horns is now in full flood at the thought of being married to 'an approved wanton'. Don Pedro, believing himself equally 'dishonoured' for having tried to 'link [his] dear friend to a common stale', adds his authority and evidence. Don John's hypocrisy lands a final blow –

> Thus, pretty lady,
> I am sorry for thy much misgovernment

– before he hurries Claudio and his brother away from the scene, leaving Hero collapsed upon the ground.

    Benedick does not go out with his friend and his prince – an obvious sign of his changed allegiance. He tries to keep calm whilst

Leonato, instantly convinced by Don Pedro of his daughter's guilt, abandons himself to bitter self-pity. Beatrice has no doubts about Hero's innocence. Friar Francis sets the weight of his training and experience against the superficial judgements that have condemned her:

> Trust not my age,
> My reverence, calling, nor divinity,
> If this sweet lady lie not guiltless here.

Leonato is half-satisfied, and falls in with the friar's scheme for deceiving Claudio into thinking that Hero is dead.

The friar's long explanation (lines 209–42) serves also to transpose the shocked feelings of an audience into a different key, ready to enjoy the moment we have all been waiting for. In her first distress Beatrice had looked for help from 'Signor Benedick', and now Benedick comes to her aid. The blank verse of tragedy changes, through the rhymed quatrain which Friar Francis speaks as he exits with Hero and Leonato, to prose for the wordplay with which Beatrice and Benedick can communicate with each other.

Very gently, they lead each other into declarations of love. Then Beatrice makes the testing demand on Benedick: 'Kill Claudio'. Benedick knows that his response will be crucial for his relationships both with Beatrice and with his former associates. The decision is soon made, and action will be taken.

SCENE 2   Meanwhile Dogberry is blundering his way through the interrogation of Conrad and Borachio until the sexton, exasperated, intervenes. He knows what happened at the wedding earlier that morning, and can confront the 'false knaves' with the truth – and with the additional information that Don John 'has secretly stolen away'. Conrad (who does not, after all, share Borachio's guilt) shakes off Dogberry's arrest with impatience – and provides Dogberry with the cue for a verbal explosion that will re-echo until his very last appearance: 'forget not that I am an ass'!

Act 5

SCENE I   Leonato's apparent grief knows no limits, and he refuses to allow Antonio to speak of any comfort until some kind of revenge is hinted. Then suddenly his attitude changes: 'My soul doth tell me Hero is belied, And that shall Claudio know . . . ' Claudio is hurrying off with Don Pedro, but Leonato, using the 'thou' form as a sign of contempt, accuses him of deceit. The two old men compete to offer a challenge against the fancy swordplay and vigour of a 'boy', but common sense and Don Pedro's authority prevail. The brothers withdraw, and the impassioned verse yields to conversational prose when Benedick enters the scene.

Don Pedro and Claudio persist in their light-hearted treatment of Benedick, not realizing the growing anger with which Benedick hears their jests. Not until he discharges himself from the company of Don Pedro, asserting Hero's innocence and Don John's guilt, does Benedick begin to persuade them to take him seriously. The truth is slow to dawn on Don Pedro (and slower still on Claudio), and the arrival of Dogberry with his prisoners causes even more suspenseful, this time comic, delay. But Borachio's confession, a simple statement of facts that attempts no excuses, makes all plain.

Verse is used once again to express Claudio's emotion as he recognizes the truth, and the irony of Leonato's accusations. Forgiveness is soon in the air, however, as Leonato prepares the way for the final deception. His brother's daughter who 'alone is heir to both of us' will marry Claudio. Claudio may be reassured even on the matter of inheritance. Borachio also reaches the dignity of verse when he generously takes all blame from Margaret. Dogberry brings everything back to prose and laughter as, rewarded for his pains, he bows out of the play with a final malapropism: 'if a merry meeting may be wished, God prohibit it'.

SCENE 2   In a happy interlude, Benedick makes a valiant attempt to compose a poem for Beatrice. Poetic language does not come easily to him – 'I was not born under a rhyming planet' – and he is more comfortable, when Beatrice enters, to resume their former contest of wit. He recognizes that they are both 'too wise to woo peaceably'.

SCENE 3   It is time for Claudio to perform his act of repentance at Hero's tomb, accompanied by Don Pedro and as many attendants, 'with tapers, all wearing mourning', as Shakespeare's dramatic company could supply to create a solemn atmosphere. Although it is short, the scene is full of genuine remorse and sorrow in the gloom of night – which is dispersed by Don Pedro's greeting of the dawn:

> Good morning, masters, put your torches out.
>   The wolves have prey'd, and look, the gentle day
> Before the wheels of Phoebus round about
>   Dapples the drowsy east with spots of grey.

A new day is dawning, and a repentant Claudio, his lines sharing the rhymes of Don Pedro's, can now prepare to meet a restored Hero.

Scene 4 A 'fair assembly' is gathering. Leonato, fully convinced of Hero's innocence, forgives Don Pedro and Claudio and receives them back into favour. Benedick, slightly embarrassed, prepares to make it a double wedding by asking permission to marry Beatrice. Claudio, eager to make amends, seems ready to 'seize upon' any of the masked ladies as a bride. Antonio repeats the simple ceremony from Act II, Scene i, lines 280–2, and 'Another Hero' stands revealed! Beatrice and Benedick's own deception is uncovered and their bickering silenced in a kiss. Benedick, urging Don Pedro to follow his example (because there is 'no staff more reverend than one tipped with horn'), leads the full company off into a final dance.

The Outsider

Messina is a world where everyone *talks*! Skill with words is essential for social survival, and a delight in language is shared by courtiers and constables alike. But Don John cannot join in: 'I am not of many words.' He reserves his angry self-mockery for the intimacy of his conversations with Conrad and Borachio, and knows that he is permanently excluded from the family togetherness that is celebrated in Leonato's 'great supper': 'Their cheer is the greater that I am subdued.'

Don John has been defeated: he had 'stood out' against his brother, his defiance failed, and the disgrace is bitter to him. It is made worse by his captive condition, 'trusted with a muzzle, and enfranchised with a clog'. The other characters look on him warily. Leonato's hospitality is conditional upon Don John's being reconciled with his brother; Beatrice claims to have indigestion – heartburn – whenever she sees him; and the gentle Hero recognizes his 'very melancholy disposition'. But there is still more to account for his isolation.

Shakespeare needed a villain who would take the place of the jealous rival of the source story of *Much Ado About Nothing* (see 'Source, Text, and Date', p.xxxi), and he found one ready-made in popular theories about psychological types: 'Bastards are envious: for he that cannot possibly mend his case will do what he can to impair others'.[1] Although Shakespeare gives Don John some reason for hating Claudio ('That young start-up hath all the glory of my overthrow'), the type figure of 'The Bastard' needed – for the Elizabethans – no further motivation for wickedness. Illegitimacy barred him from the inheritance and respect enjoyed by his legitimate brother. And the presence of such a character stands as a constant threat to the stability of a society which is grounded in marriage and family values, and where the joyful tears of Claudio's uncle are seen as 'A kind overflow of kindness' (family feeling).

---

[1] Francis Bacon, 'Of Envy' (*Essays*, 1625).

Perhaps sixteenth- and seventeenth-century audiences (without theatre programmes or cast lists) would have been able to guess Don John's illegitimacy from his appearance – possibly even bearing the 'bend sinister' (a diagonal band from left to right) on his military standard as he makes his way home from the battle. Apart from the stage directions, however, there is no reference to Don John's birth in the text of the play until Benedick, defending his friends even though he has deserted them, lays the blame for Hero's betrayal where it belongs. All three of the noblemen joined in the denunciation of Hero, he says, but

> Two of them have the very bent of honour,
> And if their wisdoms be misled in this
> The practice of it lives in John the Bastard,
> Whose spirits toil in frame of villainies.

> (Act IV, Scene i, lines 185–8)

Don John vanishes from Messina after the cruelty of the abandoned wedding and, although we hear in the very last lines of the play that he has been arrested, we are no longer interested in his fate. The evil he represented has been banished, and the 'brave punishments' that Benedick promises can wait until tomorrow: today is for dancing – 'love's proper exercise'.[2]

Shakespeare's plays have two other memorable 'Bastards' – Philip Falconbridge in *King John*, and Edmund, the bastard son of Gloucester, in *King Lear*. As if to justify his villainy, Edmund gives a most articulate – even sympathetic – statement of his 'case':

> Why bastard? Wherefore base?
> When my dimensions are as well compact,
> My mind as generous, and my shape as true
> As honest madam's issue? Why brand they us
> With base? with baseness? bastardy? base, base?
> Who in the lusty stealth of nature take
> More composition and fierce quality
> Than doth, within a dull, stale, tired bed,
> Go to th'creating a whole tribe of fops
> Got 'tween asleep and wake?

> (*King Lear*, Act I, Scene ii, lines 6–15)

---

[2] Sir John Davies, *Orchestra, or a Poem of Dancing* (1596, stanza 18):
This wondrous miracle did Love devise,
For dancing is love's proper exercise.

His words express the popular Elizabethan belief in the superior
physical and intellectual energy of the illegitimate child – qualities
Shakespeare demonstrated in Philip the Bastard, who asserts that
if he looked like his brother, Robert Falconbridge –

> And if my legs were two such riding-rods
> My arms such eel-skins stuff'd, my face so thin
> That in mine ear I durst not stick a rose
> Lest men should say 'Look, where three-farthings
>   goes!'
> And, to his shape, were heir to all this land

> (*King John*, Act I, Scene i, lines 140–4)

– he would rather be the man he is, full of life and energy.

Shakespeare's Style

Much Ado About Nothing, unlike most of Shakespeare's plays, is written largely in prose – a highly skilled, witty prose which seems to spring spontaneously from each character's imagination, and which is a great delight for the actors who speak it. Images seem to grow by free association, and are tossed from one speaker to another, caught and developed before being passed on again. The language can be colloquial or formal (but is almost always courteous), and changes from the learned to the familiar even within a phrase. This is perfect for the comedy scenes, where two or more characters, at ease with themselves and their companions, compete to be the most entertaining:

> **Benedick**
> I have almost matter enough in me for such an embassage. And so I commit you –

> **Claudio**
> To the tuition of God. From my house, if I had it –

> **Don Pedro**
> The sixth of July, your loving friend, Benedick.

> **Benedick**
> Nay, mock not, mock not. The body of your discourse is sometime guarded with fragments, and the guards are but slightly basted on neither. Ere you flout old ends any further, examine your conscience. And so I leave you.

(Act I, Scene i, lines 255–63)

Benedick's irony exaggerates Don Pedro's little errand into an 'embassage', but the formality of his leave-taking is turned against him. Claudio seizes on the word 'commit' and, backed by Don Pedro, develops it into a conventional letter-ending. Benedick, rebuking them for mockery, juggles with another idea whose relevance is not obvious until he has finished and revealed the pun on 'ends' – the endings of letters, and the leftover scraps of fabric that a tailor would use to trim a garment.

Although prose is suitable for most occasions, verse has an even greater range and flexibility when the subject is delicate or deeply felt, or when the speaker is of high rank or serious in intent. In *Much Ado*, the romantic (and near-tragic) love affair of Claudio and Hero is conducted in blank verse, the form in which most of Shakespeare's plays and those of his contemporaries are written. It is a very flexible medium, capable – like the human speaking voice – of a wide range of tones. The lines, called 'iambic pentameters', are unrhymed and have ten syllables with alternating stresses (the natural rhythm of English speech). The rhythm of the pentameter is shown in the first scene of the play when Claudio takes Don Pedro into his confidence. A perfectly regular iambic pentameter would have stresses in the following places. Notice how many of them sound like the normal rhythm of speech.

Claudio
My liége, your híghness nów may dó me góod.

Don Pedro
My lóve is thíne to téach. Teach ít but hów
And thóu shalt sée how ápt it ís to léarn
Any hard lésson thát may dó thee góod.

Claudio
Hath Léonáto ány són, my lórd?

Don Pedro
No chíld but Héro. Shé's his ónly héir.
Dost thóu afféct her, Cláudio?

Claudio
                              Ó my lórd,
When yóu went ónward ón this énded áction
I lóok'd upón her wíth a sóldier's éye,
That lík'd, but hád a róugher tásk in hánd
Than tó drive líking tó the náme of lóve.
But nów I ám retúrn'd, and thát war-thóughts
Have léft their pláces vácant, ín their róoms
Come thrónging sóft and délicáte desíres,
All prómpting mé how fáir young Héro ís,
Saying I lík'd her ére I wént to wárs.

(Act I, Scene i, lines 264–79)

At the beginning of his career Shakespeare wrote regular, 'end-stopped', lines. This means that the unit of meaning was contained within the line (as in the last two lines of this quotation). In *Much Ado About Nothing* the verse is smooth and the sense flows easily between the lines, only broken by a gentle mid-line pause (a 'caesura'). Two (or more) speakers may share a line, whether they are in agreement or at odds with each other, and this makes for a natural and speedy delivery.

Easily the best way to understand and appreciate Shakespeare's verse is to read it aloud! Don't become trapped by the dominant rhythm, but decide which are the most important words in each line and use the metre to drive them forward to the listeners.

Source, Text, and Date

Shakespeare found many versions of the story of Claudio and Hero, but his main source for the play was a tale by Matteo Bandello which was published in 1554 and which Shakespeare probably read in the original Italian.

It is a tale of love and friendship – male friendship. Sir Timbreo, a rich courtier and a favourite of the King of Aragon, falls in love with Fenicia, the daughter of a nobleman of Messina, and a marriage is arranged through the marriage-broker. But a scheme to prevent this is devised by Timbreo's friend, Girondo, who is himself in love with the girl. Timbreo is brought to witness an unknown man climbing a ladder into Fenicia's house, and his immediate reaction (still acting through a go-between) is to cancel the wedding plans. On hearing the bad news, Fenicia falls into a swoon and is believed to be dead. When she revives she is sent away into the country by her father – who never doubts his daughter's innocence but thinks that there are financial reasons for Timbreo's rejection of her. A mock funeral is held, and an empty coffin is placed in the family vault. Timbreo, who has begun to realize his evidence was flimsy, is overcome with remorse, Girondo confesses everything, and both men ask Fenicia's father for his forgiveness. A second bride, said to be Fenicia's even more beautiful sister, is married to Timbreo and proves (of course) to be Fenicia herself. Her real sister stands ready to become the wife of Girondo, now fully reconciled with Timbreo.

Shakespeare pays little attention to the 'love-versus-friendship' aspect of this story – perhaps because in earlier plays (such as *Two Gentlemen of Verona*) he had found its conventions to be artificial and unconvincing. Instead he develops Claudio's friend into the character of Benedick, giving him his own relationship with Beatrice, a personality entirely of Shakespeare's creation.

A single Quarto, published in 1600, gives the authoritative text for *Much Ado About Nothing*. This seems to have been printed from Shakespeare's own manuscript (not from a theatrical copy), and shows the dramatist still at work, leaving some loose ends and several lines that are neither verse nor prose. The stage directions and speech prefixes are sometimes uncertain or irregular – and sometimes unusually informative. Directions and speech prefixes identifying Dogberry as 'Ke' and 'Andrew' (i.e. 'Merry Andrew', the name given to a stage buffoon) show Shakespeare designing the character on and for the company's leading comic actor, Will Kemp. The prefix 'Cowley' for Verges points to another comedian, Richard Cowley, whose spindly frame and pale complexion would contrast with Kemp's burly agility.

The present edition makes use of the text established by Sheldon P. Zitner in 1993 for the Oxford Shakespeare (World's Classics).

The play is not mentioned in *Palladis Tamia*, Francis Meres's list of the best contemporary English writing, which was entered for publication in the Stationers' Register in September 1598, but the date of composition cannot have been much later than this, since Will Kemp had left the company, the Lord Chamberlain's Men, when he started a much-publicized jig from London to Norwich on 11 February 1599.

Love
Deception

Much Ado
About Nothing

Noting
counterfeiting

Characters in the Play

Don Pedro	*Prince of Aragon*
Don John	*his illegitimate brother*
Claudio	*a young lord of Florence*
Benedick	*a young lord of Padua*
Conrad } **Borachio** }	*followers of* Don John
Balthasar	*a singer, attendant upon* Don Pedro

Leonato	*Governor of Messina*
Antonio	*his brother*
Hero	Leonato's *daughter*
Beatrice	Leonato's *niece*
Margaret } **Ursula** }	*Gentlewomen attending upon* Hero

Friar Francis	*a priest*
Dogberry	*master constable*
Verges	*headborough,* Dogberry's *assistant*

Watchmen, a Sexton, a lord, messengers

Most of the action takes place outside, inside, and around the house and garden of Leonato, *Governor of Messina*

Act I

Leonato welcomes Don Pedro to his house. Beatrice engages with Benedick in a battle of wits, Claudio declares his love for Hero, and Don Pedro proposes a stratagem.

3 *three leagues*: i.e. about nine miles, or fourteen kilometres.

5 *action*: battle.

6 *sort*: rank.
   none of name: no one you would know, no one important.

11 *equally remembered*: properly rewarded.

17 *an uncle*: The uncle is never mentioned again.

Scene I

Enter Leonato, *governor of Messina*, Hero *his daughter, and* Beatrice *his niece, with a* Messenger

Leonato
I learn in this letter that Don Pedro of Aragon comes this night to Messina.

Messenger
He is very near by this. He was not three leagues off when I left him.

Leonato
5 How many gentlemen have you lost in this action?

Messenger
But few of any sort, and none of name.

Leonato
A victory is twice itself when the achiever brings home full numbers. I find here that Don Pedro hath bestowed much honour on a young Florentine called
10 Claudio.

Messenger
Much deserved on his part, and equally remembered by Don Pedro. He hath borne himself beyond the promise of his age, doing in the figure of a lamb the feats of a lion. He hath indeed better bettered
15 expectation than you must expect of me to tell you how.

Leonato
He hath an uncle here in Messina will be very much glad of it.

Messenger
I have already delivered him letters, and there
20 appears much joy in him, even so much that joy

21 *modest*: moderate.

21–2 *a badge of bitterness*: i.e. a tear, the sign of grief; badges worn by servants indicated their status and their master's rank. The Messenger's elaborate formality confuses Leonato for a moment.

25 *kind . . . kindness*: Leonato attempts a feeble pun on the different senses of 'kind' (= generous, natural, humane, or kinship).

28 *Montanto*: Beatrice coins the name (with obvious sexual innuendo) from a fencing term for an upward thrust.

31 *sort*: rank.

34 *pleasant*: amusing.

35 *bills*: advertisements.
36 *at the flight*: to an archery competition: Benedick has claimed to be a better lady-killer than Cupid.
37 *subscribed for*: responded on behalf of.
38 *bird-bolt*: blunt wooden-headed arrow used for stunning birds (given to children and fools).

41 *tax*: criticize.
42 *be meet*: get even.

44 *holp*: helped.
45 *valiant trencherman*: hearty eater.
46 *stomach*: appetite, courage.

48 *to a lord*: compared to, faced with.

---

could not show itself modest enough without a badge of bitterness.

Leonato
Did he break out into tears?

Messenger
In great measure.

Leonato
25 A kind overflow of kindness; there are no faces truer than those that are so washed. How much better is it to weep at joy than to joy at weeping!

Beatrice
I pray you, is Signor Montanto returned from the wars, or no?

Messenger
30 I know none of that name, lady. There was none such in the army, of any sort.

Leonato
What is he that you ask for, niece?

Hero
My cousin means Signor Benedick of Padua.

Messenger
O, he's returned, and as pleasant as ever he was.

Beatrice
35 He set up his bills here in Messina, and challenged Cupid at the flight; and my uncle's fool, reading the challenge, subscribed for Cupid and challenged him at the bird-bolt. I pray you, how many hath he killed and eaten in these wars? But how many hath he
40 killed? For indeed I promised to eat all of his killing.

Leonato
Faith, niece, you tax Signor Benedick too much. But he'll be meet with you, I doubt it not.

Messenger
He hath done good service, lady, in these wars.

Beatrice
You had musty victual, and he hath holp to eat it. He
45 is a very valiant trencherman; he hath an excellent stomach.

Messenger
And a good soldier too, lady.

Beatrice
And a good soldier to a lady, but what is he to a lord?

49 *stuffed with*: full of.

51 *stuffed man*: i.e. scarecrow.

58 *five wits*: Philosophers distinguished five separate mental faculties: imagination, fancy, judgement, memory, and common sense (which moderated all the others).

60–1 *for a difference*: as a heraldic mark indicating the junior branch of the family (the horse here would be the senior and superior).

62–3 *reasonable creature*: The capacity for reason is what differentiates man from all other animals.

63 *companion*: mate.

66 *faith*: i.e. the faith he has just sworn to his latest 'brother'.

67 *ever*: always.

67–8 *next block*: newest mould.

69 *books*: good books, favour.

70 *An*: if.
    study: library.

72 *squarer*: hooligan.

78 *presently*: immediately.

80 *a*: he.

Messenger
A lord to a lord, a man to a man, stuffed with all
50 honourable virtues.
Beatrice
It is so, indeed. He is no less than a stuffed man. But
for the stuffing—well, we are all mortal.
Leonato
You must not, sir, mistake my niece. There is a kind
of merry war betwixt Signor Benedick and her. They
55 never meet but there's a skirmish of wit between
them.
Beatrice
Alas, he gets nothing by that. In our last conflict four
of his five wits went halting off, and now is the whole
man governed with one; so that if he have wit
60 enough to keep himself warm, let him bear it for a
difference between himself and his horse, for it is all
the wealth that he hath left to be known a reasonable
creature. Who is his companion now? He hath every
month a new sworn brother.
Messenger
65 Is't possible?
Beatrice
Very easily possible. He wears his faith but as the
fashion of his hat; it ever changes with the next
block.
Messenger
I see, lady, the gentleman is not in your books.
Beatrice
70 No. An he were, I would burn my study. But I pray
you, who is his companion? Is there no young
squarer now that will make a voyage with him to the
devil?
Messenger
He is most in the company of the right noble
75 Claudio.
Beatrice
O Lord, he will hang upon him like a disease. He is
sooner caught than the pestilence, and the taker runs
presently mad. God help the noble Claudio. If he
have caught the Benedick, it will cost him a thousand
80 pound ere a be cured.

Messenger
I will hold friends with you, lady.
    Beatrice
Do, good friend.
    Leonato
You will never run mad, niece.
    Beatrice
No, not till a hot January.
    Messenger
85 Don Pedro is approached.

    Enter Don Pedro, Claudio, Benedick,
    Balthasar, *and* Don John *the Bastard*

    Don Pedro
Good Signor Leonato, are you come to meet your
trouble? The fashion of the world is to avoid cost,
and you encounter it.
    Leonato
Never came trouble to my house in the likeness of
90 your grace; for trouble being gone, comfort should
remain. But when you depart from me, sorrow
abides and happiness takes his leave.
    Don Pedro
You embrace your charge too willingly. I think this is
your daughter.
    Leonato
95 Her mother hath many times told me so.
    Benedick
Were you in doubt, sir, that you asked her?
    Leonato
Signor Benedick, no, for then were you a child.
    Don Pedro
You have it full, Benedick. We may guess by this
what you are, being a man. Truly, the lady fathers
100 herself. Be happy, lady, for you are like an
honourable father.

    Speaks privately with Leonato

    Benedick
If Signor Leonato be her father, she would not have
his head on her shoulders for all Messina, as like him
as she is.

---

85 *is approached*: is approaching.
85s.d. *the Bastard*: The description shows Shakespeare's first conception of this character—the text of the play makes no reference to Don John's illegitimacy until *4*, *1*, *187* (see 'The Outsider', p.xxiii).

99 *what you are*: i.e. a womanizer.
99–100 *fathers herself*: i.e. in her resemblance to Leonato.

103 *his head*: i.e. because he is bearded and has grey hair.

Beatrice

105 I wonder that you will still be talking, Signor Benedick; nobody marks you.

Benedick

What, my dear Lady Disdain! Are you yet living?

Beatrice

Is it possible disdain should die while she hath such meet food to feed it as Signor Benedick? Courtesy

110 itself must convert to disdain if you come in her presence.

Benedick

Then is courtesy a turncoat. But it is certain I am loved of all ladies, only you excepted. And I would I could find in my heart that I had not a hard heart,

115 for truly I love none.

Beatrice

A dear happiness to women. They would else have been troubled with a pernicious suitor. I thank God and my cold blood I am of your humour for that. I had rather hear my dog bark at a crow than a man

120 swear he loves me.

Benedick

God keep your ladyship still in that mind. So some gentleman or other shall scape a predestinate scratched face.

Beatrice

Scratching could not make it worse an 'twere such a

125 face as yours were.

Benedick

Well, you are a rare parrot-teacher.

Beatrice

A bird of my tongue is better than a beast of yours.

Benedick

I would my horse had the speed of your tongue, and so good a continuer. But keep your way, o' God's

130 name. I have done.

Beatrice

You always end with a jade's trick. I know you of old.

Don Pedro

[*Ending his talk with* Leonato] That is the sum of all, Leonato.—Signor Claudio and Signor Benedick, my dear friend Leonato hath invited you all. I tell him

---

109 *meet*: appropriate (and with a pun on 'meat').

116 *dear happiness*: precious piece of luck.

118 *of your . . . that*: of your frame of mind on that point.

127 *A bird . . . yours*: i.e. 'My talking bird is better than your dumb beast.'
128–9 *I would . . . continuer*: 'I wish my horse went as fast as your tongue and could go on so long.'
131 *with . . . trick*: i.e. like a stubborn horse refusing to go on.

135 we shall stay here at the least a month, and he
heartily prays some occasion may detain us longer. I
dare swear he is no hypocrite, but prays from his
heart.

Leonato

If you swear, my lord, you shall not be forsworn. [*To*
140 Don John] Let me bid you welcome, my lord. Being
reconciled to the prince your brother, I owe you all
duty.

Don John

I thank you. I am not of many words, but I thank
you.

Leonato

145 [*To* Don Pedro] Please it your grace lead on?

Don Pedro

Your hand, Leonato. We will go together.

[*Exeunt all but* Benedick *and* Claudio

Claudio

Benedick, didst thou note the daughter of Signor
Leonato?

Benedick

I noted her not, but I looked on her.

Claudio

150 Is she not a modest young lady?

Benedick

Do you question me as an honest man should do, for
my simple true judgement, or would you have me
speak after my custom, as being a professed tyrant to
their sex?

Claudio

155 No, I pray thee speak in sober judgement.

Benedick

Why, i' faith, methinks she's too low for a high
praise, too brown for a fair praise, and too little for a
great praise. Only this commendation I can afford
her, that were she other than she is she were
160 unhandsome, and being no other but as she is, I do
not like her.

Claudio

Thou thinkest I am in sport. I pray thee tell me truly
how thou likest her.

140 *Being*: since you are.

149 *noted her not*: paid no special attention to her.

153 *after my custom*: Benedick admits that his misogyny is not entirely serious. *professed*: declared.

156 *low*: short.

Benedick

Would you buy her, that you enquire after her?

Claudio

165 Can the world buy such a jewel?

Benedick

Yea, and a case to put it into. But speak you this with a sad brow, or do you play the flouting Jack, to tell us Cupid is a good hare-finder and Vulcan a rare carpenter? Come, in what key shall a man take you 170 to go in the song?

Claudio

In mine eye she is the sweetest lady that ever I looked on.

Benedick

I can see yet without spectacles, and I see no such matter. There's her cousin, an she were not 175 possessed with a fury, exceeds her as much in beauty as the first of May doth the last of December. But I hope you have no intent to turn husband, have you?

Claudio

I would scarce trust myself though I had sworn the contrary, if Hero would be my wife.

Benedick

180 Is't come to this? In faith, hath not the world one man but he will wear his cap with suspicion? Shall I never see a bachelor of three-score again? Go to, i' faith, an thou wilt needs thrust thy neck into a yoke, wear the print of it, and sigh away Sundays. Look, 185 Don Pedro is returned to seek you.

167 *sad*: serious.
   flouting Jack: scornful fellow.
168–9 *Cupid . . . carpenter*: Cupid in fact was blind, and Vulcan was a blacksmith.
169–70 *key . . . song*: musical key to sing with you, mood to understand you.

174 *cousin*: The word was used loosely for any family connection; the exact relationship between Beatrice and Hero is never explained.
   an: if.

181 *wear . . . suspicion*: wear a cap because he suspects his head has sprouted the horns of a cuckold (= the husband of an unfaithful wife).
184 *sigh away Sundays*: i.e. because he cannot go out with his male companions.

Enter Don Pedro

Don Pedro
What secret hath held you here that you followed not
to Leonato's?

Benedick
I would your grace would constrain me to tell.

Don Pedro
I charge thee on thy allegiance.

Benedick
190 You hear, Count Claudio? I can be secret as a dumb
man; I would have you think so. But on my
allegiance, mark you this—on my allegiance—he is
in love! With who? Now that is your grace's part.
Mark how short his answer is—with Hero, Leonato's
195 short daughter.

Claudio
If this were so, so were it uttered.

Benedick
Like the old tale, my lord: 'It is not so, nor 'twas not
so, but indeed, God forbid it should be so.'

Claudio
If my passion change not shortly, God forbid it
200 should be otherwise.

Don Pedro
Amen, if you love her, for the lady is very well
worthy.

Claudio
You speak this to fetch me in, my lord.

Don Pedro
By my troth, I speak my thought.

Claudio
205 And in faith, my lord, I spoke mine.

Benedick
And by my two faiths and troths, my lord, I spoke
mine.

Claudio
That I love her, I feel.

Don Pedro
That she is worthy, I know.

188 *would*: wish.

189 *charge . . . allegiance*: Benedick's sworn
allegiance to Don Pedro would override
other loyalties.

197 *old tale*: Benedick refers to a folktale of
a robber-bridegroom whose crimes were
discovered by his bride.

203 *fetch me in*: trick me into a confession.

206 *my two . . . troths*: dual loyalties—to
Don Pedro and to Claudio.

213–14 *heretic . . . beauty*: The conventions of courtly love became a 'religion' which demanded that all its adherents should at all times honour and serve the beauty of their ladies.

215 *maintain his part*: argue his position (with sexual innuendo).

215–16 *in . . . will*: through stubborn determination.

219–20 *I will . . . baldric*: 'I will wear in my forehead a horn for summoning hounds, or hang my hunting-horn in an invisible belt'—i.e. 'risk being known as a cuckold, or try to hide the fact that I have been cuckolded'.

223 *fine*: conclusion.

225 *pale with love*: Sighs of love were said to deplete the blood.

229 *ballad*: Most ballads—then as now—were about love.

234 *hang . . . cat*: A cat suspended in a leather bottle or basket was sometimes used as a target for archery practice.

236 *called Adam*: Adam Bell was a famous archer.

Benedick

210 That I neither feel how she should be loved nor know how she should be worthy is the opinion that fire cannot melt out of me. I will die in it at the stake.

Don Pedro

Thou wast ever an obstinate heretic in the despite of beauty.

Claudio

215 And never could maintain his part but in the force of his will.

Benedick

That a woman conceived me, I thank her. That she brought me up, I likewise give her most humble thanks. But that I will have a recheat winded in my

220 forehead, or hang my bugle in an invisible baldric, all women shall pardon me. Because I will not do them the wrong to mistrust any, I will do myself the right to trust none. And the fine is—for the which I may go the finer—I will live a bachelor.

Don Pedro

225 I shall see thee ere I die look pale with love.

Benedick

With anger, with sickness, or with hunger, my lord; not with love. Prove that ever I lose more blood with love than I will get again with drinking, pick out mine eyes with a ballad-maker's pen and hang me up

230 at the door of a brothel house for the sign of blind Cupid.

Don Pedro

Well, if ever thou dost fall from this faith thou wilt prove a notable argument.

Benedick

If I do, hang me in a bottle like a cat, and shoot at

235 me, and he that hits me, let him be clapped on the shoulder and called Adam.

Don Pedro

Well, as time shall try. 'In time the savage bull doth bear the yoke.'

Benedick

The savage bull may, but if ever the sensible

240 Benedick bear it, pluck off the bull's horns and set them in my forehead, and let me be vilely painted, and in such great letters as they write 'Here is good

245–6 *horn-mad*: mad as a charging bull (with the obvious allusion to the cuckold's horns).

247 *spent . . . quiver*: used up all his arrows.
Venice: The city was renowned (in Elizabethan England) for sexual licence.
250 *temporize . . . hours*: weaken as time goes by.
255 *matter*: understanding.
256 *I commit you*: Benedick parodies the formal closing of a letter.
257 *tuition*: safe-keeping.
From my house: i.e. the address from which he is writing.
259 *body*: substance, basic fabric (Benedick's imagery is from tailoring).
260 *guarded*: decorated.
261 *basted on*: loosely tacked on.

262 *flout*: scoff at.
ends: tags, quotations.
264 *My liege . . . good*: Changing the mood and subject, Claudio shifts the scene into blank verse.
268 *any son*: i.e. an heir.
270 *affect*: love.

horse to hire', let them signify under my sign 'Here you may see Benedick, the married man.'

Claudio

245 If this should ever happen thou wouldst be horn-mad.

Don Pedro

Nay, if Cupid have not spent all his quiver in Venice, thou wilt quake for this shortly.

Benedick

I look for an earthquake too, then.

Don Pedro

250 Well, you will temporize with the hours. In the meantime, good Signor Benedick, repair to Leonato's. Commend me to him, and tell him I will not fail him at supper, for indeed he hath made great preparation.

Benedick

255 I have almost matter enough in me for such an embassage. And so I commit you—

Claudio

To the tuition of God. From my house, if I had it—

Don Pedro

The sixth of July, your loving friend, Benedick.

Benedick

Nay, mock not, mock not. The body of your
260 discourse is sometime guarded with fragments, and the guards are but slightly basted on neither. Ere you flout old ends any further, examine your conscience. And so I leave you.   [*Exit*

Claudio

My liege, your highness now may do me good.

Don Pedro

265 My love is thine to teach. Teach it but how
And thou shalt see how apt it is to learn
Any hard lesson that may do thee good.

Claudio

Hath Leonato any son, my lord?

Don Pedro

No child but Hero. She's his only heir.
270 Dost thou affect her, Claudio?

Claudio
                                    O my lord,
When you went onward on this ended action
I look'd upon her with a soldier's eye,
That lik'd, but had a rougher task in hand
Than to drive liking to the name of love.
275 But now I am return'd, and that war-thoughts
Have left their places vacant, in their rooms
Come thronging soft and delicate desires,
All prompting me how fair young Hero is,
Saying I lik'd her ere I went to wars.
Don Pedro
280 Thou wilt be like a lover presently,
And tire the hearer with a book of words.
If thou dost love fair Hero, cherish it,
And I will break with her and with her father,
And thou shalt have her. Was't not to this end
285 That thou began'st to twist so fine a story?
Claudio
How sweetly you do minister to love
That know love's grief by his complexion.
But lest my liking might too sudden seem,
I would have salv'd it with a longer treatise.
Don Pedro
290 What need the bridge much broader than the flood?
The fairest grant is the necessity.
Look what will serve is fit. 'Tis once. Thou lovest,
And I will fit thee with the remedy.
I know we shall have revelling tonight.
295 I will assume thy part in some disguise,
And tell fair Hero I am Claudio.
And in her bosom I'll unclasp my heart
And take her hearing prisoner with the force
And strong encounter of my amorous tale.
300 Then after to her father will I break,
And the conclusion is, she shall be thine.
In practice let us put it presently.   [*Exeunt*

281 *book of words*: collection of love poems (conventionally required of lovers).

283 *break with*: raise the matter with.

287 *complexion*: appearance.

289 *I would . . . treatise*: 'I wanted to give a fuller account of it.'

290 *flood*: river.
291 *The . . . necessity*: 'The best gift is the one you want.'
292 *Look what*: whatever.
once: enough.

297 *in her bosom*: privately.
unclasp: open; fine books were often fastened with clasps.

Act 1   Scene 2

The first mistake: Leonato is told that Don Pedro will woo Hero for himself.

1 *my cousin*: This cousin is never mentioned again in the play.

6 *As . . . them*: 'as time will tell'.
8 *Thick-pleached alley*: path hedged in by closely interwoven branches.

10 *discovered*: revealed.
13 *accordant*: in agreement.

13–14 *take . . . top*: seize the opportunity (an allusion to the proverb 'Take Occasion by the forelock, for she is bald behind').

Scene 2

Enter Leonato, *meeting old* Antonio, *his brother*

Leonato
How now, brother, where is my cousin, your son? Hath he provided this music?

Antonio
He is very busy about it. But brother, I can tell you strange news that you yet dreamt not of.

Leonato
5 Are they good?

Antonio
As the event stamps them. But they have a good cover; they show well outward. The prince and Count Claudio, walking in a thick-pleached alley in mine orchard, were thus much overheard by a man
10 of mine: the prince discovered to Claudio that he loved my niece, your daughter, and meant to acknowledge it this night in a dance and, if he found her accordant, he meant to take the present time by the top and instantly break with you of it.

Leonato
15 Hath the fellow any wit that told you this?

Antonio

A good sharp fellow. I will send for him, and question him yourself.

Leonato

No, no. We will hold it as a dream till it appear itself. But I will acquaint my daughter withal, that she may
20 be the better prepared for an answer if peradventure this be true. Go you and tell her of it.

Enter Attendants

Cousins, you know what you have to do.—O, I cry you mercy, friend. Go you with me and I will use your skill.—Good cousin, have a care this busy time.

[*Exeunt*

Act I   Scene 3

Don John learns that Don Pedro is going to woo Hero on Claudio's behalf.

1 *What the goodyear*: Conrad uses a mild oath.
2 *measure*: proportion.

7 *sufferance*: endurance.

9 *born under Saturn*: The planet was believed to have a malign influence.
10 *mortifying mischief*: shameful disgrace (i.e. his defeat by Don Pedro, present captivity—and also, perhaps, illegitimate birth).

15 *claw . . . humour*: pander to nobody's fancy.

Scene 3

Enter Don John *the Bastard and* Conrad, *his companion*

Conrad

What the goodyear, my lord. Why are you thus out of measure sad?

Don John

There is no measure in the occasion that breeds it; therefore the sadness is without limit.

Conrad

5 You should hear reason.

Don John

And when I have heard it, what blessing brings it?

Conrad

If not a present remedy, at least a patient sufferance.

Don John

I wonder that thou, being—as thou say'st thou art—born under Saturn, goest about to apply a moral
10 medicine to a mortifying mischief. I cannot hide what I am. I must be sad when I have cause, and smile at no man's jests; eat when I have stomach, and wait for no man's leisure; sleep when I am drowsy, and tend on no man's business; laugh when
15 I am merry, and claw no man in his humour.

Conrad

Yea, but you must not make the full show of this till you may do it without controlment. You have of late stood out against your brother, and he hath ta'en you newly into his grace, where it is impossible you should take true root but by the fair weather that you make yourself. It is needful that you frame the season for your own harvest.

Don John

I had rather be a canker in a hedge than a rose in his grace. And it better fits my blood to be disdained of all than to fashion a carriage to rob love from any. In this, though I cannot be said to be a flattering honest man, it must not be denied but I am a plain-dealing villain. I am trusted with a muzzle, and enfranchised with a clog. Therefore I have decreed not to sing in my cage. If I had my mouth I would bite. If I had my liberty I would do my liking. In the meantime, let me be that I am, and seek not to alter me.

Conrad

Can you make no use of your discontent?

Don John

I make all use of it, for I use it only. Who comes here?

Enter Borachio

What news, Borachio?

Borachio

I came yonder from a great supper. The prince your brother is royally entertained by Leonato, and I can give you intelligence of an intended marriage.

Don John

Will it serve for any model to build mischief on? What is he for a fool that betroths himself to unquietness?

Borachio

Marry, it is your brother's right hand.

Don John

Who, the most exquisite Claudio?

Borachio

Even he.

20

25

30

35

40

45

20 *fair weather*: favourable opportunities.

23 *canker*: dog-rose, wild rose—*also* evil, diseased growth.
24 *blood*: temperament, [illegitimate] birth.
25 *fashion a carriage*: pretend a manner.
28–9 *enfranchised . . . clog*: set free with a weight fastened on my leg.

34 *use it only*: am *always* discontented.
36 *Borachio*: The name is from the Spanish for 'wine-bottle'.
39 *intelligence*: information.
40 *model*: ground-plan (architectural).

46 *proper squire*: fine young gentleman
    (Don John is contemptuous).

49 *forward*: precocious.
    March chick: bird hatched very early.

50 *entertained for*: hired as.
    perfumer: The Elizabethans used
    aromatic herbs as air-fresheners.

51 *comes me*: along comes; 'me' here is a
    so-called 'ethical dative', which
    functions only to intensify the verb.

53 *arras*: decorative tapestry hung before
    the wall, providing insulation—and a
    hiding-place; perhaps the conversation
    has been repeated (see *1, 2, 8note*), or
    perhaps Shakespeare has forgotten its
    location.

58 *cross*: frustrate, impede.

59 *bless*: i.e. by making the sign of the
    cross.
    sure: safe, loyal.

63 *subdued*: depressed *and* suppressed.

63–4 *o' my mind*: had the same—probably
    poisonous—thoughts as I have.

64 *prove*: find out.

Don John

A proper squire. And who, and who? Which way looks he?

Borachio

Marry, on Hero, the daughter and heir of Leonato.

Don John

A very forward March chick. How came you to this?

Borachio

50 Being entertained for a perfumer, as I was smoking a musty room, comes me the prince and Claudio, hand in hand, in sad conference. I whipped me behind the arras, and there heard it agreed upon that the prince should woo Hero for himself and, having

55 obtained her, give her to Count Claudio.

Don John

Come, come, let us thither. This may prove food to my displeasure. That young start-up hath all the glory of my overthrow. If I can cross him any way, I bless myself every way. You are both sure, and will

60 assist me?

Conrad

To the death, my lord.

Don John

Let us to the great supper. Their cheer is the greater that I am subdued. Would the cook were o' my mind. Shall we go prove what's to be done?

Borachio

65 We'll wait upon your lordship.   [*Exeunt*

Act 2

Act 2   Scene 1

The family comes together after supper and, all wearing masks, join their guests in a dance. Don Pedro talks of love to Hero; Benedick is abused by Beatrice; Claudio is misled by Don John. The mistake is corrected, Claudio is betrothed to Hero, and Don Pedro forms a plan to trick Beatrice and Benedick into falling in love with each other.

1 *here at supper*: See *1*, 3, 62: Don John must have been too late for the meal.

8 *image*: statue.
9 *my lady's . . . son*: i.e. a spoiled child.

13–14 *money . . . purse*: The words probably carry sexual innuendo ('money' = semen).
15 *a*: he.

17 *shrewd*: sharp, astringent.

18 *curst*: sarcastic.

Scene 1

Enter Leonato, Antonio *his brother,* Hero *his daughter, and* Beatrice *his niece*

Leonato
Was not Count John here at supper?

Antonio
I saw him not.

Beatrice
How tartly that gentleman looks. I never can see him but I am heartburned an hour after.

Hero
5 He is of a very melancholy disposition.

Beatrice
He were an excellent man that were made just in the midway between him and Benedick. The one is too like an image and says nothing, and the other too like my lady's eldest son, evermore tattling.

Leonato
10 Then half Signor Benedick's tongue in Count John's mouth, and half Count John's melancholy in Signor Benedick's face—

Beatrice
With a good leg and a good foot, uncle, and money enough in his purse, such a man would win any
15 woman in the world, if a could get her good will.

Leonato
By my troth, niece, thou wilt never get thee a husband if thou be so shrewd of thy tongue.

Antonio
In faith, she's too curst.

Beatrice

Too curst is more than curst. I shall lessen God's
20 sending that way, for it is said God sends a curst cow
short horns, but to a cow too curst he sends none.

Leonato

So, by being too curst, God will send you no horns.

Beatrice

Just, if he send me no husband; for the which
blessing I am at him upon my knees every morning
25 and evening. Lord, I could not endure a husband
with a beard on his face. I had rather lie in the
woollen.

Leonato

You may light on a husband that hath no beard.

Beatrice

What should I do with him? Dress him in my apparel
30 and make him my waiting gentlewoman? He that
hath a beard is more than a youth, and he that hath
no beard is less than a man; and he that is more than
a youth is not for me, and he that is less than a man,
I am not for him. Therefore I will even take sixpence
35 in earnest of the bearherd and lead his apes into hell.

Leonato

Well then, go you into hell?

Beatrice

No, but to the gate, and there will the devil meet me
like an old cuckold with horns on his head, and say,
'Get you to heaven, Beatrice, get you to heaven.
40 Here's no place for you maids.' So deliver I up my
apes, and away to Saint Peter fore the heavens. He
shows me where the bachelors sit, and there live we
as merry as the day is long.

Antonio

[*To* Hero] Well, niece, I trust you will be ruled by
45 your father.

Beatrice

Yes, faith, it is my cousin's duty to make curtsy and
say, 'Father, as it please you.' But yet for all that,
cousin, let him be a handsome fellow, or else make
another curtsy and say, 'Father, as it please me.'

Leonato

50 Well, niece, I hope to see you one day fitted with a
husband.

20–1 *God . . . horns*: A proverbial expression: the 'curst cow' can do little harm with short horns.

23 *no husband*: Talk of 'horns' inevitably leads to thoughts of cuckoldry—even among ladies.

26–7 *lie . . . woollen*: sleep between blankets (without sheets).

35 *in earnest*: as a down payment on a contract.
bearherd: animal showman (who kept bears for baiting and other creatures for show).
lead . . . hell: Proverbially said to be the fate of unmarried women (although the expression has never been satisfactorily explained).

41 *Saint Peter*: the keeper of the gates of heaven (Matthew 16:19).
fore the heavens: outside the gate of heaven; the Folio's reading ('for the heavens') could also be an interjection or a mild oath.

42 *bachelors*: The word was then applied to both sexes.

52 *mettle*: material—with a pun on 'mettle' = spirit.
53 *earth*: 'God formed man of the dust of the ground' (Genesis 2:7).
55 *marl*: clay.
56–7 *Adam's . . . kindred*: Beatrice argues that all men must be descended from Adam (the first man), and therefore related; but the church forbids the marriage of close relatives.

62 *in good time*: at the appropriate moment *and* in the proper rhythm.
   important: importunate, demanding.
63 *measure*: proportion *and* rhythm.

69 *ancientry*: tradition.
70 *bad legs*: perhaps caused by old age.
   cinquepace: Beatrice can pun on the name (pronounced 'sink-apace') of this dance (a sequence of five steps followed by a great leap).
72 *passing*: very.
75s.d. *don masks*: In a pretence of anonymity (which would permit a more free conversation), the Elizabethans wore elaborate, often grotesque, face masks in their festivities.

77 *a bout*: a turn about the dance floor.
78 *friend*: lover.

Beatrice

Not till God make men of some other mettle than earth. Would it not grieve a woman to be overmastered with a piece of valiant dust, to make an 55 account of her life to a clod of wayward marl? No, uncle, I'll none. Adam's sons are my brethren, and truly I hold it a sin to match in my kindred.

Leonato

[*To* Hero] Daughter, remember what I told you. If the prince do solicit you in that kind, you know your 60 answer.

Beatrice

The fault will be in the music, cousin, if you be not wooed in good time. If the prince be too important, tell him there is measure in everything, and so dance out the answer. For hear me, Hero, wooing, 65 wedding, and repenting is as a Scotch jig, a measure, and a cinquepace. The first suit is hot and hasty, like a Scotch jig and full as fantastical; the wedding mannerly modest, as a measure, full of state and ancientry. And then comes repentance, and with his 70 bad legs falls into the cinquepace faster and faster till he sink into his grave.

Leonato

Cousin, you apprehend passing shrewdly.

Beatrice

I have a good eye, uncle; I can see a church by daylight.

Leonato

75 [*To* Antonio] The revellers are entering, brother.

He signals to the others to disperse and don masks

Make good room.

Enter Don Pedro, Claudio, Benedick, Balthasar, [Margaret *and* Ursula], *all masked;* Don John *and* Borachio, [*unmasked*]; *and* Attendants *and* Musicians, *among them a drummer*

Don Pedro

[*To* Hero] Lady, will you walk a bout with your friend?

Hero

So you walk softly, and look sweetly, and say
80 nothing, I am yours for the walk; and especially
when I walk away.

Don Pedro

With me in your company?

Hero

I may say so when I please.

Don Pedro

And when please you to say so?

Hero

85 When I like your favour; for God defend the lute
should be like the case.

Don Pedro

My visor is Philemon's roof.
Within the house is Jove.

Hero

Why, then, your visor should be thatched.

Don Pedro

90 Speak low if you speak love.

They move aside

Balthasar

[*To* Margaret] Well, I would you did like me.

Margaret

So would not I for your own sake, for I have many ill
qualities.

Balthasar

Which is one?

Margaret

95 I say my prayers aloud.

Balthasar

I love you the better; the hearers may cry amen.

Margaret

God match me with a good dancer.

Balthasar

Amen.

Margaret

And God keep him out of my sight when the dance
100 is done. Answer, clerk.

Balthasar

No more words. The clerk is answered.

85 *favour*: face.
   defend: forbid.
86 *case*: Don Pedro was probably wearing a
   grotesque mask.
87 *Philemon*: A peasant who, with his wife
   Baucis, entertained the gods unawares
   in their humble cottage; the story is told
   in Ovid's *Metamorphoses,* which was
   translated by Arthur Golding into
   English rhymed verse with fourteen
   syllables—imitated here in lines 87–90.
89 *thatched*: i.e. like the roof of Philemon's
   cottage.

100 *clerk*: The parish clerk made responses
    to the priest.
101 *answered*: Balthasar has understood
    Margaret's rejection.

They move aside

Ursula
[*To* Antonio] I know you well enough, you are Signor
Antonio.

Antonio
At a word, I am not.

Ursula
105 I know you by the waggling of your head.

Antonio
To tell you true, I counterfeit him.

Ursula
You could never do him so ill-well unless you were
the very man. Here's his dry hand up and down. You
are he, you are he.

Antonio
110 At a word, I am not.

Ursula
Come, come, do you think I do not know you by your
excellent wit? Can virtue hide itself? Go to, mum,
you are he. Graces will appear, and there's an end.

They move aside

Beatrice
[*To* Benedick] Will you not tell me who told you so?

Benedick
115 No, you shall pardon me.

Beatrice
Nor will you not tell me who you are?

Benedick
Not now.

Beatrice
That I was disdainful, and that I had my good wit
out of the 'Hundred Merry Tales'—well, this was
120 Signor Benedick that said so.

Benedick
What's he?

Beatrice
I am sure you know him well enough.

Benedick
Not I, believe me.

Beatrice
Did he never make you laugh?

108   *dry*: withered.
   up and down: exactly.

112   *mum*: be quiet, no more talk.

119   *Hundred Merry Tales*: a collection of
   comic anecdotes, first published in 1526
   and reprinted many times.

Benedick

125 I pray you, what is he?

Beatrice

126–7 *Only his gift*: his only talent.

Why, he is the prince's jester, a very dull fool. Only his gift is in devising impossible slanders. None but libertines delight in him, and the commendation is not in his wit but in his villainy, for he both pleases

129–30 *pleases . . . them*: amuses some men (by abusing others) and angers those he slanders.
131 *fleet*: company, assembly.
132 *boarded me*: tried it on with me.

130 men and angers them, and then they laugh at him and beat him. I am sure he is in the fleet. I would he had boarded me.

Benedick

When I know the gentleman, I'll tell him what you say.

Beatrice

135 *break a comparison*: See below, lines 221–42.
136 *peradventure*: perhaps.

135 Do, do. He'll but break a comparison or two on me, which peradventure not marked, or not laughed at, strikes him into melancholy, and then there's a partridge wing saved, for the fool will eat no supper that night. [*Music*] We must follow the leaders.

Benedick

140 In every good thing.

Beatrice

Nay, if they lead to any ill I will leave them at the next turning.

They dance off.

[*Exeunt all but* Don John, Borachio, *and* Claudio

Don John

143 *amorous on*: in love with.

[*Aside to* Borachio] Sure my brother is amorous on Hero, and hath withdrawn her father to break with

145 him about it. The ladies follow her, and but one visor remains.

146 *visor*: mask.

Borachio

[*Aside to* Don John] And that is Claudio. I know him by his bearing.

Don John

[*Approaching* Claudio] Are not you Signor Benedick?

Claudio

150 You know me well. I am he.

Don John

151 *near . . . love*: intimate with my brother.

Signor, you are very near my brother in his love. He is enamoured on Hero. I pray you dissuade him from

her. She is no equal for his birth. You may do the
part of an honest man in it.

Claudio

155 How know you he loves her?

Don John

I heard him swear his affection.

Borachio

So did I, too, and he swore he would marry her
tonight.

Don John

Come, let us to the banquet.

[*Exeunt all but* Claudio

Claudio

160 Thus answer I in name of Benedick,
But hear these ill news with the ears of Claudio.
'Tis certain so; the prince woos for himself.
Friendship is constant in all other things
Save in the office and affairs of love.

165 Therefore all hearts in love use their own tongues.
Let every eye negotiate for itself,
And trust no agent; for beauty is a witch
Against whose charms faith melteth into blood.
This is an accident of hourly proof,

170 Which I mistrusted not. Farewell, therefore, Hero.

Enter Benedick

Benedick

Count Claudio?

Claudio

Yea, the same.

Benedick

Come, will you go with me?

Claudio

Whither?

Benedick

175 Even to the next willow, about your own business,
County. What fashion will you wear the garland of?
About your neck, like an usurer's chain? Or under
your arm, like a lieutenant's scarf? You must wear it
one way, for the prince hath got your Hero.

Claudio

180 I wish him joy of her.

159 *banquet*: a dessert course of wine, fruit,
and sweets served after the dancing.
165 *all hearts . . . tongues*: let all lovers speak
for themselves.
168 *faith*: loyalty.
blood: sexual desire.
169 *accident . . . proof*: something that
happens all the time.
170 *mistrusted not*: did not suspect.
175 *willow*: The willow tree was an emblem
of unrequited love.

176 *County*: count; the variant has no
significance.
176–8 *What . . . scarf*: i.e. 'What are you
going to do about it—demand
compensation or challenge the prince to
a duel?'
177 *usurer's chain*: the rich gold chain worn
by a moneylender.
178 *lieutenant's scarf*: military sash worn
diagonally from the shoulder to denote
rank.

181 *drover*: cattle-dealer.

Benedick
Why, that's spoken like an honest drover; so they sell bullocks. But did you think the prince would have served you thus?

Claudio
I pray you leave me.

Benedick
185 Ho, now you strike like the blind man. 'Twas the boy that stole your meat, and you'll beat the post.

Claudio
If it will not be, I'll leave you.   [*Exit*

Benedick
Alas, poor hurt fowl, now will he creep into sedges.—But that my Lady Beatrice should know 190 me, and not know me! The prince's fool! Ha, it may be I go under that title because I am merry. Yea, but so I am apt to do myself wrong. I am not so reputed! It is the base and bitter disposition of Beatrice that puts the world into her person, and so gives me out. 195 Well, I'll be revenged as I may.

Enter Don Pedro

Don Pedro
Now, signor, where's the count? Did you see him?

Benedick
Troth, my lord, I have played the part of Lady Fame. I found him here as melancholy as a lodge in a warren. I told him—and I think I told him true— 200 that your grace had got the good will of this young lady, and I offered him my company to a willow tree, either to make him a garland, as being forsaken, or to bind him up a rod, as being worthy to be whipped.

Don Pedro
To be whipped? What's his fault?

Benedick
205 The flat transgression of a schoolboy who, being overjoyed with finding a bird's nest, shows it his companion, and he steals it.

Don Pedro
Wilt thou make a trust a transgression? The transgression is in the stealer.

185–6 *strike . . . post*: hit out wildly; the allusion is to a Spanish story (translated into English in 1586) about a servant who deceived his cruel master, a blind man, into hitting a pillar.

187 *If . . . be*: if you won't leave me.

192 *so*: i.e. I being merry.

194 *puts . . . person*: thinks everybody shares her opinions.
gives me out: reports me.

197 *Lady Fame*: the personification of rumour.

198–9 *lodge . . . warren*: game-keeper's hovel in a park (whose loneliness might encourage melancholy).

205 *flat*: certain, undeniable.

214 *them*: i.e. the birds.

216 *their singing . . . saying*: they sing what you say you have taught them.

226 *a great thaw*: This might be 'dull' because it kept everyone indoors.

227 *impossible conveyance*: incredible skill.

228 *at a mark*: next to an archery target (signalling the results).

229 *poniards*: daggers.

230 *her terminations*: the pointed endings of her sentences, her terms (of abuse).

233–4 *all . . . transgressed*: i.e. the whole earth (which Adam forfeited when he fell from God's grace—Genesis, chapter 3).

234–6 *She would . . . too*: Hercules, the superman of classical mythology, was forced by Omphale to wear women's clothing and to spin cloth whilst she took away his club and the lion skin which he wore.

235 *turned spit*: turned the handle of the spit (for roasting meat).

237 *Ate . . . apparel*: The goddess of Discord, who (traditionally) was well dressed.

237–8 *some scholar . . . her*: some learned man (knowing Latin) would cast the devil out of her.

Benedick

210 Yet it had not been amiss the rod had been made, and the garland too, for the garland he might have worn himself, and the rod he might have bestowed on you, who, as I take it, have stolen his bird's nest.

Don Pedro

I will but teach them to sing, and restore them to the 215 owner.

Benedick

If their singing answer your saying, by my faith you say honestly.

Don Pedro

The Lady Beatrice hath a quarrel to you. The gentleman that danced with her told her she is much 220 wronged by you.

Benedick

O, she misused me past the endurance of a block. An oak but with one green leaf on it would have answered her. My very visor began to assume life and scold with her. She told me, not thinking I had 225 been myself, that I was the prince's jester, that I was duller than a great thaw, huddling jest upon jest with such impossible conveyance upon me that I stood like a man at a mark, with a whole army shooting at me. She speaks poniards, and every word stabs. If 230 her breath were as terrible as her terminations, there were no living near her; she would infect to the North Star. I would not marry her though she were endowed with all that Adam had left him before he transgressed. She would have made Hercules have 235 turned spit, yea, and have cleft his club to make the fire, too. Come, talk not of her. You shall find her the infernal Ate in good apparel. I would to God some scholar would conjure her, for certainly, while she is here a man may live as quiet in hell as in a sanctuary, 240 and people sin upon purpose because they would go thither. So indeed all disquiet, horror, and perturbation follows her.

244–50 *Will your grace . . . pigmies*: Benedick's list of impossible tasks combines travellers' tales with traditional love trials.

247 *tooth-picker*: Toothpicks, a fashionable Italian innovation, made ideal travel souvenirs.

248 *Prester John*: a legendary king supposed to rule a Christian country in Africa or Asia.

249 *Great Cham*: Kubla Khan, sovereign Prince of Tartary.

250 *pigmies*: legendary dwarfs living in Ethiopia and the Far East (the African peoples had not yet been discovered).

251 *harpy*: The harpies (in classical mythology) were malevolent birds with the faces of women.

258–61 *he lent . . . lost it*: Beatrice hints at an earlier relationship with Benedick.

259 *use for*: interest on.
double: i.e. Beatrice (not being possessive in her love) returned Benedick's heart when she gave him her own.

260 *Marry*: by [the Virgin] Mary; a mild oath.

262 *put him down*: got the better of him (in wit).

264–5 *So . . . fools*: Beatrice understands a literal sense to Don Pedro's words.

Enter Claudio *and* Beatrice

Don Pedro
Look, here she comes.

Benedick
Will your grace command me any service to the
245 world's end? I will go on the slightest errand now to
the Antipodes that you can devise to send me on. I
will fetch you a tooth-picker now from the furthest
inch of Asia, bring you the length of Prester John's
foot, fetch you a hair off the Great Cham's beard, do
250 you any embassage to the pigmies, rather than hold
three words' conference with this harpy. You have no
employment for me?

Don Pedro
None but to desire your good company.

Benedick
O God, sir, here's a dish I love not. I cannot endure
255 my Lady Tongue.   [*Exit*

Don Pedro
Come, lady, come, you have lost the heart of Signor
Benedick.

Beatrice
Indeed, my lord, he lent it me a while, and I gave
him use for it, a double heart for his single one.
260 Marry, once before he won it of me with false dice.
Therefore your grace may well say I have lost it.

Don Pedro
You have put him down, lady, you have put him
down.

Beatrice
So I would not he should do me, my lord, lest I
265 should prove the mother of fools. I have brought
Count Claudio, whom you sent me to seek.

Don Pedro
Why, how now, Count, wherefore are you sad?

Claudio
Not sad, my lord.

Don Pedro
How then? Sick?

Claudio
270 Neither, my lord.

also p. 66

*Orange - yellow
→ jealousy*

Beatrice

The count is neither sad, nor sick, nor merry, nor well, but civil count, civil as an orange, and something of that jealous complexion.

Don Pedro

I' faith, lady, I think your blazon to be true, though
275 I'll be sworn, if he be so, his conceit is false. Here, Claudio, I have wooed in thy name, and fair Hero is won. I have broke with her father and his good will obtained.

> Don Pedro *signals*; enter Leonato *with* Hero

Name the day of marriage, and God give thee joy.

Leonato

280 Count, take of me my daughter, and with her my fortunes. His grace hath made the match, and all grace say amen to it.

Beatrice

Speak, Count, 'tis your cue.

Claudio

Silence is the perfectest herald of joy. I were but little
285 happy if I could say how much. [*To* Hero] Lady, as you are mine, I am yours. I give away myself for you, and dote upon the exchange.

Beatrice

[*To* Hero] Speak, cousin; or, if you cannot, stop his mouth with a kiss, and let not him speak, neither.

Don Pedro

290 In faith, lady, you have a merry heart.

Beatrice

Yea, my lord. I thank it, poor fool, it keeps on the windy side of care.—My cousin tells him in his ear that he is in her heart.

Claudio

And so she doth, cousin.

Beatrice

295 Good Lord, for alliance! Thus goes everyone to the world but I, and I am sunburnt. I may sit in a corner and cry 'Heigh-ho for a husband.'

Don Pedro

Lady Beatrice, I will get you one.

272   *civil*: A pun with 'Seville' leads to the thought of bitter oranges and the colour—yellow—of jealousy.

274   *blazon*: heraldic description.

275   *conceit*: notion, understanding.

277   *broke with*: spoken to.

280–2   *Count . . . to it*: Leonato's formal language makes this engagement official and binding—a 'marriage by pre-contract'.

291   *poor fool*: poor old thing.

292   *windy . . . care*: upwind of trouble.

295   *Good . . . alliance*: Beatrice reacts to Claudio's 'cousin' (line 294).

295–6   *Thus . . . world*: that's the way of the world for everyone.

296   *sunburnt*: A suntan was unfashionable and undesirable in Elizabethan England.

297   *cry . . . husband*: go whistle for a husband.

Beatrice

I would rather have one of your father's getting. Hath
300 your grace ne'er a brother like you? Your father got
excellent husbands if a maid could come by them.

Don Pedro

Will you have me, lady?

Beatrice

No, my lord, unless I might have another for
working days. Your grace is too costly to wear every
305 day. But I beseech your grace, pardon me; I was
born to speak all mirth and no matter.

Don Pedro

Your silence most offends me, and to be merry best
becomes you; for out o' question, you were born in
a merry hour.

Beatrice

310 No, sure, my lord, my mother cried. But then there
was a star danced, and under that was I born. [*To*
Hero *and* Claudio] Cousins, God give you joy.

Leonato

Niece, will you look to those things I told you of?

Beatrice

I cry you mercy, uncle. [*To* Don Pedro] By your
315 grace's pardon.   [*Exit* Beatrice

Don Pedro

By my troth, a pleasant-spirited lady.

Leonato

There's little of the melancholy element in her, my
lord. She is never sad but when she sleeps, and not
ever sad then; for I have heard my daughter say she
320 hath often dreamt of unhappiness and waked herself
with laughing.

Don Pedro

She cannot endure to hear tell of a husband.

Leonato

O, by no means. She mocks all her wooers out of
suit.

Don Pedro

325 She were an excellent wife for Benedick.

Leonato

O Lord! My lord, if they were but a week married
they would talk themselves mad.

---

299 *getting*: begetting.

310 *cried*: in labour.

317 *melancholy element*: i.e. black bile;
human beings were thought to be made
up of four elements (blood, phlegm,
and choler were the others), and the
dominance of any one of these
determined the individual
temperament.
318 *sad*: serious.
319 *ever*: always.
323–4 *out of suit*: out of courtship.

Don Pedro

County Claudio, when mean you to go to church?

Claudio

Tomorrow, my lord. Time goes on crutches till love
330 have all his rites.

Leonato

Not till Monday, my dear son, which is hence a just
sevennight; and a time too brief, too, to have all
things answer my mind.

Don Pedro

Come, you shake the head at so long a breathing, but
335 I warrant thee, Claudio, the time shall not go dully
by us. I will in the interim undertake one of
Hercules' labours, which is to bring Signor Benedick
and the Lady Beatrice into a mountain of affection
th'one with th'other. I would fain have it a match,
340 and I doubt not but to fashion it, if you three will but
minister such assistance as I shall give you direction.

Leonato

My lord, I am for you, though it cost me ten nights'
watchings.

Claudio

And I, my lord.

Don Pedro

345 And you too, gentle Hero?

Hero

I will do any modest office, my lord, to help my
cousin to a good husband.

Don Pedro

And Benedick is not the unhopefullest husband that
I know. Thus far can I praise him: he is of a noble
350 strain, of approved valour and confirmed honesty. I
will teach you how to humour your cousin that she
shall fall in love with Benedick; and I, with your two
helps, will so practise on Benedick that, in despite of
his quick wit and his queasy stomach, he shall fall in
355 love with Beatrice. If we can do this, Cupid is no
longer an archer; his glory shall be ours, for we are
the only love-gods. Go in with me, and I will tell you
my drift. _Treiben_   [*Exeunt*

331–2 _a just sevennight_: exactly a week.

333 _answer my mind_: just as I want them.

334 _breathing_: pause, delay.

336 _interim_: meantime.

337 _Hercules' labours_: The demi-god of classical mythology demonstrated his divine nature by accomplishing twelve near-impossible tasks.

339 _would fain_: would like to.

342–3 _nights' watchings_: sleepless nights.

350 _strain_: lineage.
approved: tested (in battle).

353 _practise on_: influence, work upon.

354 _queasy stomach_: This would give him little appetite (for marriage).

358 _drift_: intentions.

Don John is delighted when Borachio proposes a scheme to discredit Hero.

schänden

3 *cross*: obstruct, thwart.

6–7 *whatsoever . . . mine*: whatever goes against his wishes goes along with mine.

20 *temper*: concoct.

23 *estimation*: merit, quality.
24 *stale*: whore.

26 *misuse*: abuse.
    vex: torment.

Scene 2

Enter Don John *and* Borachio

Don John
It is so. The Count Claudio shall marry the daughter of Leonato.

Borachio
Yea, my lord, but I can cross it.

Don John
Any bar, any cross, any impediment will be
5 medicinable to me. I am sick in displeasure to him, and whatsoever comes athwart his affection ranges evenly with mine. How canst thou cross this marriage?

Borachio
Not honestly, my lord, but so covertly that no
10 dishonesty shall appear in me.

Don John
Show me briefly how.

Borachio
I think I told your lordship a year since how much I am in the favour of Margaret, the waiting gentlewoman to Hero.

Don John
15 I remember.

Borachio
I can at any unseasonable instant of the night appoint her to look out at her lady's chamber window.

Don John
What life is in that to be the death of this marriage?

Borachio
20 The poison of that lies in you to temper. Go you to the prince your brother. Spare not to tell him that he hath wronged his honour in marrying the renowned Claudio—whose estimation do you mightily hold up—to a contaminated stale, such a one as Hero.

Don John
25 What proof shall I make of that?

Borachio
Proof enough to misuse the prince, to vex Claudio, to undo Hero and kill Leonato. Look you for any other issue?

Dohn John & Borachio
have planed to make it look
as if ~~Borachio~~ Hero would cheat on Claudio with Borachio

ACT 2 SCENE 2   31

29 *Only*: for no other reason but.

30 *meet*: fitting.

32 *Intend*: pretend.

35 *cozened*: deceived, cheated.
36 *semblance of a maid*: i.e. a virgin in
     appearance only.
37 *discovered*: revealed.
38–9 *Offer . . . likelihood*: give them
     examples which will be no more
     unlikely.

45 *jealousy*: suspicion.
46 *assurance*: proof.

48 *cunning*: clever.

Don John
Only to despite them I will endeavour anything.
Borachio
30 Go then. Find me a meet hour to draw Don Pedro
and the Count Claudio alone. Tell them that you
know that Hero loves me. Intend a kind of zeal both
to the prince and Claudio—as in love of your
brother's honour who hath made this match, and his
35 friend's reputation who is thus like to be cozened
with the semblance of a maid—that you have
discovered thus. They will scarcely believe this
without trial. Offer them instances, which shall bear
no less likelihood than to see me at her chamber
40 window, hear me call Margaret Hero, hear Margaret
term me Claudio. And bring them to see this the
very night before the intended wedding, for in the
meantime I will so fashion the matter that Hero shall
be absent, and there shall appear such seeming truth
45 of Hero's disloyalty that jealousy shall be called
assurance, and all the preparation overthrown.
Don John
Grow this to what adverse issue it can, I will put it in
practice. Be cunning in the working of this, and thy
fee is a thousand ducats.
Borachio
50 Be you constant in the accusation, and my cunning
shall not shame me.
Don John
I will presently go learn their day of marriage.

[*Exeunt*

Benedick talks about Claudio and how he has changed

Act 2   Scene 3

Benedick is tricked into believing that
Beatrice is in love with him.

5   *I . . . already*: I'll be back immediately:
but Benedick deliberately
misunderstands.

11   *argument*: subject.

13   *drum . . . fife*: i.e. military music.

14   *tabor*: small drum usually played on
festival occasions.

übezeugt

17   *carving*: designing.
     doublet: garment, with detachable
sleeves, for man's upper body.

20   *orthography*: rhetorician.

22   *converted*: transformed.

25   *oyster*: i.e. the lowest form of animal life
(in the Elizabethan hierarchy).

31   *cheapen*: make a bid for.

32   *Noble*: Benedick couples the usual sense
with the name of a coin (33p in today's
money).

33   *angel*: coin worth 50p.

Scene 3

Enter Benedick

Benedick

Boy!

Enter Boy

Boy

Signor?

Benedick

In my chamber window lies a book. Bring it hither to
me in the orchard.

Boy

5   I am here already, sir.

Benedick

I know that, but I would have thee *dahr* hence and here
again. [*Exit* Boy] I do much wonder that one man,
seeing how much another man is a fool when he
dedicates his behaviours to love, will, after he hath
10   laughed at such shallow follies in others, become the
argument of his own scorn by *(Veracchtung)* falling in love. And
such a man is Claudio. I have known when there was
no music with him but the drum and the fife, and
now had he rather hear the tabor and the pipe. I have
15   known when he would have walked ten mile afoot to
see a good armour, and now will he lie ten nights
awake carving the fashion of a new doublet. He was
wont to speak plain and to the purpose, like an
honest man and a soldier, and now is he turned
20   orthography. His words are a very fantastical
banquet, just so many strange dishes. May I be so
umgewandelt converted and see with these eyes? I cannot tell; I
think not. I will not be sworn but love may transform
me to an oyster. But I'll take my oath on it: till he
25   have made an oyster of me he shall never make me
such a fool. One woman is fair, yet I am well.
Another is wise, yet I am well. Another virtuous, yet
I am well. But till all graces be in one woman, one
woman shall not come in my *(Gnade)* grace. Rich she shall
30   be, that's certain. Wise, or I'll none. Virtuous, or I'll
never cheapen her. Fair, or I'll never look on her.
Mild, or come not near me. Noble, or not I for an
angel. Of good discourse, an excellent musician, and

Gespräch

her hair shall be of what colour it please God.—Ha!
35 The prince and Monsieur Love. I will hide me in the
arbour.

> *He hides. Enter* Don Pedro, Leonato, *and*
> Claudio

Don Pedro
Come, shall we hear this music?
   Claudio
Yea, my good lord. How still the evening is,
As hush'd on purpose to grace harmony.
   Don Pedro
40 [*Aside*] See you where Benedick hath hid himself?
   Claudio
[*Aside*] O, very well, my lord. The music ended,
We'll fit the hid fox with a pennyworth.

> *Enter* Balthasar *with music*

Don Pedro
Come, Balthasar, we'll hear that song again.
   Balthasar
O good my lord, tax not so bad a voice
45 To slander music any more than once.
   Don Pedro
It is the witness still of excellency
To put a strange face on his own perfection.
I pray thee sing, and let me woo no more.
   Balthasar
Because you talk of wooing I will sing,
50 Since many a wooer doth commence his suit
To her he thinks not worthy, yet he woos.
Yet will he swear he loves.
   Don Pedro
               Nay, pray thee, come;
Or if thou wilt hold longer argument,
Do it in notes.
   Balthasar
          Note this before my notes:
55 There's not a note of mine that's worth the noting.
   Don Pedro
Why, these are very crotchets that he speaks.
Note notes, forsooth, and nothing!

42 *pennyworth*: value for his money.

44 *tax*: make demands on.

46 *witness*: proof, evidence.
   still: always.
47 *put . . . on*: pretend not to recognize.

56 *crotchets*: quarter notes *and*
eccentricities.
57 *nothing*: nothing else; Don Pedro is tired
of Balthasar's quibbling.

The accompaniment begins

Benedick

Now, divine air! Now is his soul ravished. Is it not
strange that sheep's guts should hale souls out of
60 men's bodies? Well, a horn for my money, when all's
done.

Balthasar

[*Sings*]

   Sigh no more, ladies, sigh no more.
      Men were deceivers ever,
   One foot in sea, and one on shore,
65   To one thing constant never.
   Then sigh not so, but let them go,
      And be you blithe and bonny,
   Converting all your sounds of woe
      Into hey nonny, nonny.

70   Sing no more ditties, sing no more
      Of dumps so dull and heavy.
   The fraud of men was ever so
      Since summer first was leafy.
   Then sigh not so, but let them go,
75   And be you blithe and bonny,
   Converting all your sounds of woe
      Into hey nonny, nonny.

Don Pedro

By my troth, a good song.

Balthasar

And an ill singer, my lord.

Don Pedro

80 Ha, no, no, faith. Thou sing'st well enough for a
shift.

Benedick

[*Aside*] An he had been a dog that should have
howled thus, they would have hanged him. And I
pray God his bad voice bode no mischief. I had as
85 lief have heard the night-raven, come what plague
could have come after it.

Don Pedro

Yea, marry, dost thou hear, Balthasar? I pray thee get
us some excellent music, for tomorrow night we
would have it at the Lady Hero's chamber window.

---

59 *sheep's guts*: i.e. a stringed instrument
(probably a lute).
hale: draw.
60 *horn*: hunting horn.

71 *dumps*: mournful melodies.

81–1 *for a shift*: as a makeshift.

82 *An*: if.

84–5 *as lief*: rather.
85 *night-raven*: a bird of ill omen.

88 *some excellent music*: This music is never
mentioned again.

Balthasar

90 The best I can, my lord.

Don Pedro

Do so. Farewell.   [*Exit* Balthasar
Come hither, Leonato. What was it you told me of
today, that your niece Beatrice was in love with
Signor Benedick?

95 *stalk on*: i.e. proceed like hunters hiding behind a stalking horse.
the fowl sits: he's a sitting duck.

Claudio

95 [*Aside*] O, ay, stalk on, stalk on; the fowl sits. [*Raising his voice*] I did never think that lady would have loved any man.

Leonato

No, nor I neither. But most wonderful that she should so dote on Signor Benedick, whom she hath
100 in all outward behaviours seemed ever to abhor.

101 *Sits . . . corner*: is that how things are.

Benedick

[*Aside*] Is't possible? Sits the wind in that corner?

Leonato

By my troth, my lord, I cannot tell what to think of it. But that she loves him with an enraged affection, it is past the infinite of thought.

104 *it is . . . thought*: i.e. no amount of thinking can understand.

Don Pedro

105 Maybe she doth but counterfeit.

Claudio

Faith, like enough.

Leonato

O God! Counterfeit? There was never counterfeit of passion came so near the life of passion as she discovers it.

109 *discovers*: shows.

Don Pedro

110 Why, what effects of passion shows she?

Claudio

[*Aside*] Bait the hook well. This fish will bite.

Leonato

What effects, my lord? She will sit you—you heard my daughter tell you how.

112 *sit you*: The 'ethical dative', used here in an attempt to arouse interest when words fail.

Claudio

She did indeed.

Don Pedro

115 How, how, I pray you? You amaze me. I would have thought her spirit had been invincible against all assaults of affection.

Leonato

I would have sworn it had, my lord, especially against Benedick.

Benedick

120 *gull*: trick.

120 [*Aside*] I should think this a gull, but that the white-bearded fellow speaks it. Knavery cannot, sure, hide himself in such reverence.

Claudio

[*Aside*] He hath ta'en th'infection. Hold it up.

Don Pedro

Hath she made her affection known to Benedick?

Leonato

125 No, and swears she never will. That's her torment.

Claudio

'Tis true, indeed, so your daughter says. 'Shall I,' says she, 'that have so oft encountered him with scorn, write to him that I love him?'

Leonato

This says she now when she is beginning to write to

131 *smock*: slip, under-garment.

130 him; for she'll be up twenty times a night, and there will she sit in her smock till she have writ a sheet of paper. My daughter tells us all.

Claudio

Now you talk of a sheet of paper, I remember a pretty jest your daughter told us of.

Leonato

135 O, when she had writ it and was reading it over, she found 'Benedick' and 'Beatrice' between the sheet.

Claudio

136 *between the sheet*: i.e. the bedsheets.

That.

137 *That*: Claudio expresses disappointment that Leonato tells such an old joke so badly.

138 *halfpence*: little coins.

Leonato

O, she tore the letter into a thousand halfpence, railed at herself that she should be so immodest to

140 write to one that she knew would flout her. 'I measure him,' says she, 'by my own spirit, for I should flout him if he writ to me. Yea, though I loved him I should.'

Claudio

Then down upon her knees she falls, weeps, sobs,

145 beats her heart, tears her hair, prays, curses. 'O sweet Benedick! God give me patience.'

Leonato

She doth indeed; my daughter says so. And the
ecstasy hath so much overborne her that my
daughter is sometime afeard she will do a desperate
150 outrage to herself. It is very true.

Don Pedro

It were good that Benedick knew of it by some other,
if she will not discover it.

Claudio

To what end? He would make but a sport of it and
torment the poor lady worse.

Don Pedro

155 An he should, it were an alms to hang him. She's an
excellent sweet lady and, out of all suspicion, she is
virtuous.

Claudio

And she is exceeding wise.

Don Pedro

In everything but in loving Benedick.

Leonato

160 O my lord, wisdom and blood combating in so
tender a body, we have ten proofs to one that blood
hath the victory. I am sorry for her, as I have just
cause, being her uncle and her guardian.

Don Pedro

I would she had bestowed this dotage on me. I
165 would have doffed all other respects and made her
half myself. I pray you tell Benedick of it, and hear
what a will say.

Leonato

Were it good, think you?

Claudio

Hero thinks surely she will die; for she says she will
170 die if he love her not, and she will die ere she make
her love known, and she will die if he woo her, rather
than she will bate one breath of her accustomed
crossness.

Don Pedro

She doth well. If she should make tender of her love
175 'tis very possible he'll scorn it, for the man, as you
know all, hath a contemptible spirit.

Claudio

He is a very proper man.

---

148 *ecstasy*: frenzy.

155 *an alms*: an act of charity.

160 *blood*: passion.

165 *doffed*: put aside.

167 *a*: he.

172 *bate*: abate.

174 *make tender of*: offer.

176 *contemptible*: contemptuous.

177 *proper*: attractive, good-looking.

178 *outward happiness*: appearance.

180 *wit*: intelligence.

182 *Hector*: the Trojan champion.

190 *large*: broad, improper.

193 *wear it out*: get over it, learn to accept things.

202 *upon*: after.

207 *no such matter*: there will be nothing in it.

Don Pedro
He hath indeed a good outward happiness.
Claudio
Before God, and in my mind, very wise.
Don Pedro
180 He doth indeed show some sparks that are like wit.
Claudio
And I take him to be valiant.
Don Pedro
As Hector, I assure you. And in the managing of quarrels you may say he is wise, for either he avoids them with great discretion or undertakes them with
185 a most Christianlike fear.
Leonato
If he do fear God, a must necessarily keep peace. If he break the peace, he ought to enter into a quarrel with fear and trembling.
Don Pedro
And so will he do, for the man doth fear God,
190 howsoever it seems not in him by some large jests he will make. Well, I am sorry for your niece. Shall we go seek Benedick and tell him of her love?
Claudio
Never tell him, my lord. Let her wear it out with good counsel.
Leonato
195 Nay, that's impossible. She may wear her heart out first.
Don Pedro
Well, we will hear further of it by your daughter. Let it cool the while. I love Benedick well, and I could wish he would modestly examine himself to see how
200 much he is unworthy so good a lady.
Leonato
My lord, will you walk? Dinner is ready.
Claudio
[*Aside*] If he do not dote on her upon this, I will never trust my expectation.
Don Pedro
[*Aside*] Let there be the same net spread for her,
205 and that must your daughter and her gentlewomen carry. The sport will be when they hold one opinion of the other's dotage, and no such matter. That's the

208–9 *dumb show*: mime (because they will be speechless with embarrassment).

211 *sadly*: seriously.

213 *have . . . bent*: are fully stretched (like a bow).

221 *reprove*: disprove, doubt.

223 *argument*: evidence.
224 *horribly*: exceedingly.

228 *meat*: food.
229 *sentences*: maxims, wise sayings.
230–1 *career of his humour*: pursuit of his inclination.

238 *Fair Beatrice . . . pains*: Benedick thanks Beatrice with a regular blank verse line.

scene that I would see, which will be merely a dumb show. Let us send her to call him in to dinner.

[*Exeunt* Don Pedro, Claudio, *and* Leonato

Benedick

210 [*Coming forward*] This can be no trick. The conference was sadly borne. They have the truth of this from Hero. They seem to pity the lady; it seems her affections have their full bent. Love me? Why, it must be requited. I hear how I am censured. They
215 say I will bear myself proudly if I perceive the love come from her. They say too that she will rather die than give any sign of affection. I did never think to marry. I must not seem proud. Happy are they that hear their detractions and can put them to mending.
220 They say the lady is fair; 'tis a truth, I can bear them witness. And virtuous; 'tis so, I cannot reprove it. And wise, but for loving me. By my troth, it is no addition to her wit nor no great argument of her folly, for I will be horribly in love with her. I may
225 chance have some odd quirks and remnants of wit broken on me because I have railed so long against marriage, but doth not the appetite alter? A man loves the meat in his youth that he cannot endure in his age. Shall quips and sentences and these paper
230 bullets of the brain awe a man from the career of his humour? No. The world must be peopled. When I said I would die a bachelor, I did not think I should live till I were married. Here comes Beatrice.

Enter Beatrice

By this day, she's a fair lady. I do spy some marks of
235 love in her.

Beatrice

Against my will I am sent to bid you come in to dinner.

Benedick

Fair Beatrice, I thank you for your pains.

Beatrice

I took no more pains for those thanks than you take
240 pains to thank me. If it had been painful I would not have come.

Benedick

You take pleasure, then, in the message?

244 *daw*: jackdaw.
244–5 *no stomach*: no appetite.

Beatrice
Yea, just so much as you may take upon a knife's point and not choke a daw withal.—You have no 245 stomach, signor? Fare you well.   [*Exit*

Benedick
Ha! 'Against my will I am sent to bid you come in to dinner.' There's a double meaning in that. 'I took no more pains for those thanks than you took pains to thank me.' That's as much as to say 'Any pains that 250 I take for you is as easy as thanks.' If I do not take pity of her I am a villain. If I do not love her I am a Jew. I will go get her picture.   [*Exit*

252 *a Jew*: i.e. have no faith.
get her picture: Benedick intends to commission a miniature portrait which he can wear, perhaps, as a locket.

Act 3

Beatrice is tricked into believing that
Benedick is in love with her.

1 *parlour*: a room reserved for private
family use.

3 *Proposing*: conversing.

4 *Ursula*: The Quarto's spelling 'Ursley'
probably reflects contemporary
pronunciation.

7 *pleached*: pleachèd. See *1*, *2*, *8*.

8–11 *Where . . . bred it*: Hero repeats one
of the moral commonplaces of her
education.

12 *propose*: conversation.

14 *presently*: immediately.

16 *trace*: pace.

23 *only wounds*: wounds only.

Scene 1

*Hero planing to
make her believe, Benedick
loves her* [handwritten annotation]

Enter Hero *and two gentlewomen,* Margaret
and Ursula

Hero
Good Margaret, run thee to the parlour.
There shalt thou find my cousin Beatrice
Proposing with the prince and Claudio.
Whisper her ear, and tell her I and Ursula
5 Walk in the orchard, and our whole discourse
Is all of her. Say that thou overheard'st us,
And bid her steal into the pleached bower
Where honeysuckles, ripened by the sun,
Forbid the sun to enter, like favourites
10 Made proud by princes, that advance their pride
Against that power that bred it. There will she hide
her
To listen our propose. This is thy office.
Bear thee well in it, and leave us alone.
Margaret
I'll make her come, I warrant you, presently.   [*Exit*
Hero
15 Now, Ursula, when Beatrice doth come,
As we do trace this alley up and down
Our talk must only be of Benedick.
When I do name him, let it be thy part
To praise him more than ever man did merit.
20 My talk to thee must be how Benedick
Is sick in love with Beatrice. Of this matter
Is little Cupid's crafty arrow made,
That only wounds by hearsay.

Enter Beatrice, *who hides*

Now begin,
For look where Beatrice like a lapwing runs
25 Close by the ground to hear our conference.
> **Ursula**
[*Aside to* Hero] The pleasant'st angling is to see the fish
Cut with her golden oars the silver stream
And greedily devour the treacherous bait.
So angle we for Beatrice, who even now
30 Is couched in the woodbine coverture.
Fear you not my part of the dialogue.
> **Hero**
[*Aside to* Ursula] Then go we near her, that her ear lose nothing
Of the false-sweet bait that we lay for it.

Approaching Beatrice's *hiding-place*

No, truly, Ursula, she is too disdainful.
35 I know her spirits are as coy and wild
As haggards of the rock.
> **Ursula**
> > But are you sure
That Benedick loves Beatrice so entirely?
> **Hero**
So says the prince and my new-trothed lord.
> **Ursula**
And did they bid you tell her of it, madam?
> **Hero**
40 They did entreat me to acquaint her of it,
But I persuaded them, if they lov'd Benedick,
To wish him wrestle with affection
And never to let Beatrice know of it.
> **Ursula**
Why did you so? Doth not the gentleman
45 Deserve as full as fortunate a bed
As ever Beatrice shall couch upon?
> **Hero**
O god of love! I know he doth deserve
As much as may be yielded to a man,
But nature never fram'd a woman's heart
50 Of prouder stuff than that of Beatrice.

24 *lapwing*: The lapwing (plover) runs along the ground to draw predators away from its nest.
25 *conference*: conversation.

30 *couched*: couchèd.
woodbine: honeysuckle.
coverture: shelter.

35 *coy*: defiant.
36 *haggards*: wild hawks.

38 *new-trothed*: trothèd; recently betrothed.

45 *as full . . . bed*: just as good a marriage.

52 *Misprising*: undervaluing.
54 *All matter . . . weak*: all other discourse seems of little worth.
55 *shape*: image.
project: idea.
56 *self-endear'd*: in love with herself.
60 *How*: however.
rarely: handsomely.
61 *spell him backward*: take everything the wrong way: Hero proceeds to demonstrate her meaning.
63 *black*: dark, swarthy.
antic: grotesque.
64 *ill-headed*: with a poor head.
65 *agate . . . cut*: Agate stones, often carved with human figures, were used on seal-rings.

66 *vane*: weather-vane.
67 *moved*: movèd.
70 *simpleness*: integrity.
purchaseth: earns.
71, 73 *commendable*: The stress is on the first syllable.
72 *from*: contrary to.
76 *press . . . wit*: heap jokes upon me until I died with laughing; pressing to death, '*peine forte et dure*', was the punishment inflicted on criminals who refused to speak when arraigned before a court.
80 *tickling*: This word needs to be pronounced with an extra syllable ('tick-el-ing') if the rhythm is to be completely regular; see 5, 4, 34.

84 *honest slanders*: harmless lies.

Disdain and scorn ride sparkling in her eyes,
Misprising what they look on, and her wit
Values itself so highly that to her
All matter else seems weak. She cannot love,
55 Nor take no shape nor project of affection,
She is so self-endear'd.
   Ursula
              Sure, I think so,
And therefore certainly it were not good
She knew his love, lest she'll make sport at it.
   Hero
Why, you speak truth. I never yet saw man,
60 How wise, how noble, young, how rarely featur'd,
But she would spell him backward. If fair-fac'd,
She would swear the gentleman should be her sister;
If black, why nature, drawing of an antic,
Made a foul blot; if tall, a lance ill-headed;
65 If low, an agate very vilely cut;
If speaking, why, a vane blown with all winds;
If silent, why, a block moved with none.
So turns she every man the wrong side out,
And never gives to truth and virtue that
70 Which simpleness and merit purchaseth.
   Ursula
Sure, sure, such carping is not commendable.
   Hero
No, not to be so odd and from all fashions
As Beatrice is cannot be commendable.
But who dare tell her so? If I should speak,
75 She would mock me into air; O, she would laugh me
Out of myself, press me to death with wit.
Therefore let Benedick, like cover'd fire,
Consume away in sighs, waste inwardly.
It were a better death than die with mocks,
80 Which is as bad as die with tickling.
   Ursula
Yet tell her of it; hear what she will say.
   Hero
No. Rather I will go to Benedick
And counsel him to fight against his passion.
And truly, I'll devise some honest slanders
85 To stain my cousin with. One doth not know

How much an ill word may empoison liking.

Ursula

O, do not do your cousin such a wrong.
She cannot be so much without true judgement,
Having so swift and excellent a wit

90 As she is priz'd to have, as to refuse
So rare a gentleman as Signor Benedick.

Hero

He is the only man of Italy,
Always excepted my dear Claudio.

Ursula

I pray you be not angry with me, madam;

95 Speaking my fancy, Signor Benedick,
For shape, for bearing, argument, and valour
Goes foremost in report through Italy.

Hero

Indeed, he hath an excellent good name.

Ursula

His excellence did earn it ere he had it.

100 When are you married, madam?

Hero

Why, every day, tomorrow. Come, go in.
I'll show thee some attires and have thy counsel
Which is the best to furnish me tomorrow.

Ursula

[*Aside*] She's lim'd, I warrant you, we have caught
her, madam.

Hero

105 [*Aside*] If it prove so, then loving goes by haps.
Some Cupid kills with arrows, some with traps.

[*Exeunt* Hero *and* Ursula

Beatrice

[*Coming forward*] What fire is in mine ears? Can this
be true?
   Stand I condemn'd for pride and scorn so much?
Contempt, farewell; and maiden pride, adieu.
110   No glory lives behind the back of such.
And, Benedick, love on. I will requite thee,
   Taming my wild heart to thy loving hand.
If thou dost love, my kindness shall incite thee
   To bind our loves up in a holy band.
115 For others say thou dost deserve, and I
Believe it better than reportingly.   [*Exit*

90 *priz'd*: esteemed.
96 *argument*: discourse.
100 *married*: to be married.
101 *every day, tomorrow*: 'for every day of
    my life—but the ceremony is
    tomorrow'.
102 *attires*: head-dresses.
104 *lim'd*: caught with bird-lime (a sticky
    substance smeared on branches where
    the birds were likely to land).

105 *haps*: chances.
107–16 *What . . . reportingly*: Beatrice, like
    Benedick at 2, 3, 238, speaks her love in
    verse (two rhyming quatrains and a
    closing couplet—almost a sonnet).
107 *What . . . ears*: A burning sensation in
    the ears is (proverbially) a sign that
    someone is talking about you.

112 *Taming . . . heart*: Beatrice remembers
    the hawk image of lines 35–6.

114 *band*: bond.

116 *reportingly*: mere hearsay.

Act 3   Scene 2

necken

Don Pedro and Claudio tease Benedick about his changed appearance, but their laughter is silenced by Don John's insinuations.

Unterstellungen

3 *bring*: escort.
  vouchsafe: permit.

9–10 *little hangman*: little scamp.

16 *truant*: rogue.

22 *hang . . . draw it*: Hanging and drawing (disembowelling) were punishments for felons.

24 *humour . . . worm*: It was believed that toothache was caused by worms breeding in the rotten moisture of a hollow tooth.

Scene 2

> *Enter* Don Pedro, Claudio, Benedick, *and* Leonato

Don Pedro
I do but stay till your marriage be consummate, and then go I toward Aragon.

Claudio
I'll bring you thither, my lord, if you'll vouchsafe me.

Don Pedro   *gleichferes*
Nay, that would be as great a soil in the new gloss of
5 your marriage as to show a child his new coat and forbid him to wear it. I will only be bold with Benedick for his company, for from the crown of his head to the sole of his foot he is all mirth. He hath twice or thrice cut Cupid's bowstring, and the little
10 hangman dare not shoot at him. He hath a heart as sound as a bell, and his tongue is the clapper, for what his heart thinks his tongue speaks.

Benedick
Kavaliere Gallants, I am not as I have been.

Leonato
So say I. Methinks you are sadder.

Claudio
15 I hope he be in love.

Don Pedro *Schurke*
Hang him, truant! There's no true drop of blood in him to be truly touched with love. If he be sad, he wants money.

Benedick
I have the toothache.

Don Pedro
20 Draw it. *ziehen lassen*

Benedick
Hang it.

Claudio
You must hang it first and draw it afterwards.

Don Pedro
What? Sigh for the toothache?

Leonato
Where is but a humour or a worm.

28 *fancy*: i.e. affection.
strange disguises: Don Pedro mocks the contemporary English trend for imitating European fashions.

31 *slops*: voluminous breeches.
40 *old . . . cheek*: Someone must have told Benedick how Beatrice said she 'could not endure a husband with a beard on his face' (2, 1, 25–6).
41 *stuffed tennis balls*: Tennis was played with leather balls stuffed with horse-hair.
44 *civet*: perfume based on musk taken from glands of the civet cat.
47 *note*: indication.
melancholy: The lover's melancholy was a recognized psychological condition.
48 *wash his face*: i.e. with perfume—after-shave lotion.
49 *paint himself*: use cosmetics.
51–2 *his . . . stops*: i.e. he has stopped joking now and started singing love-songs.
52 *by stops*: with frets (like a lute-string).

Benedick
25 Well, everyone can master a grief but he that has it.

Claudio
Yet say I he is in love.

Don Pedro
There is no appearance of fancy in him, unless it be a fancy that he hath to strange disguises: as to be a Dutchman today, a Frenchman tomorrow, or in the
30 shape of two countries at once, as a German from the waist downward, all slops, and a Spaniard from the hip upward, no doublet. Unless he have a fancy to this foolery, as it appears he hath, he is no fool for fancy, as you would have it appear he is.

Claudio
35 If he be not in love with some woman, there is no believing old signs. A brushes his hat o' mornings; what should that bode?

Don Pedro
Hath any man seen him at the barber's?

Claudio
No, but the barber's man hath been seen with him,
40 and the old ornament of his cheek hath already stuffed tennis balls.

Leonato
Indeed, he looks younger than he did by the loss of a beard.

Don Pedro
Nay, a rubs himself with civet. Can you smell him
45 out by that?

Claudio
That's as much as to say the sweet youth's in love.

Don Pedro
The greatest note of it is his melancholy.

Claudio
And when was he wont to wash his face?

Don Pedro
Yea, or to paint himself? For the which I hear what
50 they say of him.

Claudio
Nay, but his jesting spirit, which is now crept into a lute-string, and now governed by stops.

Don Pedro
Indeed, that tells a heavy tale for him. Conclude,
conclude, he is in love.
Claudio
55 Nay, but I know who loves him.
Don Pedro
That would I know, too. I warrant, one that knows
him not.
Claudio
Yes, and his ill conditions, and in despite of all, dies
for him.
Don Pedro
60 She shall be buried with her face upwards.
Benedick
Yet is this no charm for the toothache. Old signor,
walk aside with me. I have studied eight or nine wise
words to speak to you which these hobby-horses
must not hear.   [*Exeunt* Benedick *and* Leonato
Don Pedro
65 For my life, to break with him about Beatrice.
Claudio
'Tis even so. Hero and Margaret have by this played
their parts with Beatrice, and then the two bears will
not bite one another when they meet.

Enter Don John *the Bastard*

Don John
My lord, and brother, God save you.
Don Pedro
70 Good-e'en, brother.
Don John
If your leisure served I would speak with you.
Don Pedro
In private?
Don John
If it please you. Yet Count Claudio may hear, for
what I would speak of concerns him.
Don Pedro
75 What's the matter?
Don John
[*To* Claudio] Means your lordship to be married
tomorrow?

58 *ill conditions*: bad qualities.
dies: i.e. in orgasm; Don Pedro's
comment in the next line shows that he
has understood the sexual innuendo.
60 *buried . . . upwards*: i.e. smothered by
Benedick.

63 *hobby-horses*: buffoons (so-called after
the stylized horse fastened round the
waist of a morris-dancer).

Don Pedro
You know he does.

Don John
I know not that when he knows what I know.

Claudio   *Hindernisse*
80 If there be any impediment, I pray you discover it.

Don John
You may think I love you not. Let that appear
hereafter, and aim better at me by that I now will
manifest. For my brother, I think he holds you well,
and in dearness of heart hath holp to effect your
85 ensuing marriage—surely suit ill spent, and labour ill
bestowed. *verlethen*   *Arbeit*
                                    Mühseligkeit
Don Pedro
Why, what's the matter?

Don John
I came hither to tell you; and, circumstances
shortened—for she has been too long a-talking of—
90 the lady is disloyal.

Claudio
Who, Hero?

Don John
Even she—Leonato's Hero, your Hero, every man's
Hero.

Claudio
Disloyal?

Don John   *Bosheit*
95 The word is too good to paint out her wickedness; I
could say she were worse. Think you of a worse title,
and I will fit her to it. Wonder not till further
warrant. Go but with me tonight, you shall see her
chamber window entered, even the night before her
100 wedding day. If you love her then, tomorrow wed
her. But it would better fit your honour to change
your mind.

Claudio
May this be so?

Don Pedro
I will not think it.

Don John
105 If you dare not trust that you see, confess not that
you know. If you will follow me I will show you

82–3 *aim . . . manifest*: judge me better
    from what I will now reveal to you.
83 *holds you well*: thinks highly of you.
84 *holp*: helped.

88–9 *circumstances shortened*: cutting a long
    story short.

95 *paint out*: give a full picture of.

105–6 *If you . . . know*: if you don't believe
    what you see, say you don't know
    anything (i.e. any reason why you
    should not be married to Hero—see
    4, 1, 11–13 *note*).

enough, and when you have seen more and heard more, proceed accordingly.

Claudio

If I see anything tonight why I should not marry her, 110 tomorrow, in the congregation where I should wed, there will I shame her.

Don Pedro

And as I wooed for thee to obtain her, I will join with thee to disgrace her.

Don John

I will disparage her no farther till you are my 115 witnesses. Bear it coldly but till midnight, and let the issue show itself.

Don Pedro

O day untowardly turned!

Claudio

O mischief strangely thwarting!

Don John

O plague right well prevented! So will you say when 120 you have seen the sequel.   [*Exeunt*

115   *coldly*: calmly.

117   *untowardly turned*: miserably transformed.

Act 3   Scene 3

The Watchmen, instructed to guard the city, overhear Borachio telling Conrad how Hero has been betrayed. An arrest is made.

os.d. *the Watch*: A number of citizens conscripted for (unpaid) police duty.

3 *salvation*: Verges means 'damnation'; such malapropisms form the characteristic speech modes of both Verges and Dogberry.

7 *charge*: duties.

8 *desertless*: Dogberry intends 'deserving'.

9 *constable*: officer responsible for maintenance of public order.

10 *A Watchman*: Neither of the early texts distinguishes in speech-prefixes between the different Watchmen—whose number would vary according to the number of available actors.

Scene 3

> *Enter* Dogberry *and his partner* Verges, *with the* Watch

Dogberry
Are you good men and true?

Verges
Yea, or else it were pity but they should suffer salvation, body and soul.

Dogberry
Nay, that were a punishment too good for them if
5 they should have any allegiance in them, being chosen for the prince's watch.

Verges
Well, give them their charge, neighbour Dogberry.

Dogberry
First, who think you the most desertless man to be constable?

A Watchman
10 Hugh Oatcake, sir, or George Seacoal, for they can write and read.

Dogberry

Come hither, neighbour Seacoal, God hath blessed you with a good name. To be a well-favoured man is the gift of fortune, but to write and read comes by
15 nature.

A Watchman

Both which, Master Constable—

Dogberry

You have. I knew it would be your answer. Well, for your favour, sir, why, give God thanks, and make no boast of it. And for your writing and reading, let that
20 appear when there is no need of such vanity. You are thought here to be the most senseless and fit man for the constable of the watch; therefore, bear you the lantern. This is your charge: you shall comprehend all vagrom men. You are to bid any man stand, in the
25 prince's name.

A Watchman

How if a will not stand?

Dogberry

Why then take no note of him, but let him go, and presently call the rest of the watch together, and thank God you are rid of a knave.

Verges

30 If he will not stand when he is bidden, he is none of the prince's subjects.

Dogberry

True, and they are to meddle with none but the prince's subjects. You shall also make no noise in the streets, for for the watch to babble and to talk is most
35 tolerable and not to be endured.

A Watchman

We will rather sleep than talk. We know what belongs to a watch.

Dogberry

Why, you speak like an ancient and most quiet watchman, for I cannot see how sleeping should
40 offend. Only have a care that your bills be not stolen. Well, you are to call at all the alehouses and bid those that are drunk get them to bed.

A Watchman

How if they will not?

---

13 *well-favoured*: good looking.

14–15 *fortune . . . nature*: Dogberry seems to be trying to oppose the concepts of 'nature' and 'nurture' popular in philosophical discussion.

24 *vagrom*: vagrant.
    stand: halt.

26 *a*: he.

32 *meddle*: be concerned with.

38 *ancient*: experienced.

40 *bills*: halberds (long-handled, axe-headed weapons).

Dogberry

Why then, let them alone till they are sober. If they
45 make you not then the better answer, you may say
they are not the men you took them for.

A Watchman

Well, sir.

Dogberry

If you meet a thief you may suspect him, by virtue of
your office, to be no true man; and for such kind of
50 men, the less you meddle or make with them, why,
the more is for your honesty.

A Watchman

If we know him to be a thief, shall we not lay hands
on him?

Dogberry

Truly, by your office you may, but I think they that
55 touch pitch will be defiled. The most peaceable way
for you if you do take a thief is to let him show
himself what he is, and steal out of your company.

Verges

You have been always called a merciful man, partner.

Dogberry

Truly, I would not hang a dog by my will, much
60 more a man who hath any honesty in him.

Verges

If you hear a child cry in the night, you must call to
the nurse and bid her still it.

A Watchman

How if the nurse be asleep and will not hear us?

Dogberry

Why then, depart in peace and let the child wake her
65 with crying, for the ewe that will not hear her lamb
when it baas will never answer a calf when he bleats.

Verges

'Tis very true.

Dogberry

This is the end of the charge. You, constable, are to
present the prince's own person. If you meet the
70 prince in the night you may stay him.

Verges

Nay, by'r Lady, that I think a cannot.

49   *true*: honest.

54–5   *they . . . defiled*: Dogberry quotes from
the Apocrypha (Ecclesiasticus 13:1).

59   *by my will*: if I had my way.

65–6   *the ewe . . . bleats*: Dogberry seems to
invent his own folk wisdom.

69   *present*: represent.

Dogberry

Five shillings to one on't with any man that knows the statutes he may stay him. Marry, not without the prince be willing, for indeed the watch ought to
75 offend no man, and it is an offence to stay a man against his will.

Verges

By'r Lady, I think it be so.

Dogberry

Ha ha ha! Well, masters, good night. An there be any matter of weight chances, call up me. Keep your
80 fellows' counsels, and your own, and good night. [*To* Verges] Come, neighbour.

A Watchman

Well, masters, we hear our charge. Let us go sit here upon the church bench till two, and then all to bed.

Dogberry

One word more, honest neighbours. I pray you
85 watch about Signor Leonato's door, for the wedding being there tomorrow, there is a great coil tonight. Adieu. Be vigitant, I beseech you.

[*Exeunt* Dogberry *and* Verges

Enter Borachio *and* Conrad

Borachio

What, Conrad!

A Watchman

[*Aside*] Peace, stir not.

Borachio

90 Conrad, I say.

Conrad

Here, man, I am at thy elbow.

Borachio

Mass, an my elbow itched, I thought there would a scab follow.

Conrad

I will owe thee an answer for that. And now, forward
95 with thy tale.

78 *Ha ha ha*: Dogberry has forced Verges to agree with him
An: if.

86 *coil*: commotion, bustle.
87 *vigitant*: vigilant.

92 *Mass*: by the mass (a mild oath).
my elbow itched: This was proverbially said to be a warning of evil or danger.
93 *scab*: scoundrel—and the result of scratching the itch.

Borachio

Stand thee close then under this penthouse, for it drizzles rain; and I will, like a true drunkard, utter all to thee.

A Watchman

[*Aside*] Some treason, masters. Yet stand close.

Borachio

100 Therefore, know I have earned of Don John a thousand ducats.

Conrad

Is it possible that any villainy should be so dear?

Borachio

Thou shouldst rather ask if it were possible any villainy should be so rich. For when rich villains have 105 need of poor ones, poor ones may make what price they will.

Conrad

I wonder at it.

Borachio

That shows thou art unconfirmed. Thou knowest that the fashion of a doublet, or a hat, or a cloak is 110 nothing to a man.

Conrad

Yes, it is apparel.

Borachio

I mean the fashion.

Conrad

Yes, the fashion is the fashion.

Borachio

Tush, I may as well say the fool's the fool. But seest 115 thou not what a deformed thief this fashion is?

A Watchman

[*Aside*] I know that Deformed. A has been a vile thief this seven year. A goes up and down like a gentleman. I remember his name.

Borachio

Didst thou not hear somebody?

Conrad

120 No, 'twas the vane on the house.

Borachio

Seest thou not, I say, what a deformed thief this fashion is, how giddily a turns about all the hot-

96 *penthouse*: overhang (probably the projection above part of the stage).
97 *a true drunkard*: i.e. truthfully (*in vino veritas*—there's truth in wine).

99 *close*: hidden.
101 *thousand ducats*: The sum was large, but not enormous; the ducat varied in value at different times and in different countries.
105 *make*: ask.
108 *unconfirmed*: inexperienced.
109–10 *is nothing . . . man*: tells you nothing *about* a man (but Conrad understands 'means nothing *to* a man').
115 *deformed*: perverse, absurd.

124-5 *Pharaoh's . . . painting*: Borachio refers to a wall-hanging in some tavern; Pharaoh's soldiers were drowned in the Red Sea when they were pursuing Moses and the Israelites (Exodus 14:23-8).

125 *reechy*: grimy.
   god Bel's priests: The priests were slain by the king of Persia after Daniel denounced them for worshipping a false god (Apocrypha: The Book of Daniel, chapter 14, Douai Bible).
126-8 *shaven Hercules . . . club*: Borachio perhaps refers to a picture of Hercules with Omphale (see *2, 1, 234-6 note*), although Hercules never lost his beard.
128 *codpiece*: decorative pouch worn at the front of a man's breeches.
131 *shifted*: changed (with a pun on shift = change clothes).
139 *possessed by*: convinced by, under the [diabolic] influence of.
146 *my villainy*: Borachio must have been questioned by Don Pedro and Claudio after his performance.
155 *lechery*: for 'treachery'.

bloods between fourteen and five-and-thirty,
sometimes fashioning them like Pharaoh's soldiers in
125 the reechy painting, sometime like god Bel's priests
in the old church window, sometime like the shaven
Hercules in the smirched, worm-eaten tapestry,
where his codpiece seems as massy as his club?

Conrad

All this I see, and I see that the fashion wears out
130 more apparel than the man. But art not thou thyself
giddy with the fashion, too, that thou hast shifted
out of thy tale into telling me of the fashion?

Borachio

Not so, neither. But know that I have tonight wooed
Margaret, the Lady Hero's gentlewoman, by the
135 name of Hero. She leans me out at her mistress'
chamber window, bids me a thousand times good
night.—I tell this tale vilely. I should first tell thee
how the prince, Claudio, and my master, planted
and placed and possessed by my master Don John,
140 saw afar off in the orchard this amiable encounter.

Conrad

And thought they Margaret was Hero?

Borachio

Two of them did, the prince and Claudio. But the
devil my master knew she was Margaret. And partly
by his oaths, which first possessed them, partly by
145 the dark night, which did deceive them, but chiefly
by my villainy, which did confirm any slander that
Don John had made—away went Claudio enraged,
swore he would meet her as he was appointed next
morning at the temple, and there, before the whole
150 congregation, shame her with what he saw o'ernight,
and send her home again without a husband.

A Watchman

[*Coming forward*] We charge you in the prince's
name. Stand!

A Watchman

Call up the right Master Constable. We have here
155 recovered the most dangerous piece of lechery that
ever was known in the commonwealth.

158 *lock*: lovelock, hanging curl (a
fashionable hairstyle at the time).

165 *commodity*: useful article, *and*, goods
obtained on credit.
taken up: received on credit, arrested.
bills: halberds, security bonds.
166 *in question*: in demand, questionable
(legally).

A Watchman
And one Deformed is one of them. I know him; a
wears a lock.
Conrad
Masters, masters—
A Watchman
160 You'll be made bring Deformed forth, I warrant you.
Conrad
Masters—
A Watchman
Never speak, we charge you. Let us obey you to go
with us.
Borachio
[*To* Conrad] We are like to prove a goodly
165 commodity, being taken up of these men's bills.
Conrad
A commodity in question, I warrant you. Come,
we'll obey you.   [*Exeunt*

Act 3   Scene 4

Hero is being dressed for her wedding—but
Beatrice has a heavy cold.

6 *Troth*: faith.
rebato: a stiff ornamented collar pinned
on to a lady's gown.

Scene 4

Enter Hero, Margaret, *and* Ursula

Hero
Good Ursula, wake my cousin Beatrice, and desire
her to rise.
Ursula
I will, lady.
Hero
And bid her come hither.
Ursula
5 Well.   [*Exit*
Margaret
Troth, I think your other rebato were better.
Hero
No, pray thee, good Meg, I'll wear this.
Margaret
By my troth, 's not so good, and I warrant your
cousin will say so.

12 *tire*: decorative head-dress (perhaps incorporating false hair and ornaments).

16 *exceeds*: beats everything.

17 *night-gown*: dressing-gown; these were often very elaborate creations of silk or satin, trimmed with fur.

18 *cuts*: slashes in the main fabric of a gown revealing even richer cloth beneath.

19 *down . . . sleeves*: tight sleeves fitted down to the wrist, and looser, fuller sleeves draped from the shoulders.

20 *underborne*: trimmed at the hem, or worn over a petticoat.

bluish tinsel: light blue silk cloth shot through with gold or silver threads.

21 *quaint*: intricate and elegant.

Hero

10 My cousin's a fool, and thou art another; I'll wear none but this.

Margaret

I like the new tire within excellently, if the hair were a thought browner. And your gown's a most rare fashion, i' faith. I saw the Duchess of Milan's gown

15 that they praise so.

Hero

O, that exceeds, they say.

Margaret

By my troth, 's but a night-gown in respect of yours—cloth o' gold, and cuts, and laced with silver, set with pearls, down sleeves, side sleeves, and skirts

20 round underborne with a bluish tinsel. But for a fine, quaint, graceful, and excellent fashion, yours is worth ten on't.

Hero

God give me joy to wear it, for my heart is exceeding heavy.

Margaret

25 'Twill be heavier soon by the weight of a man.

Hero

Fie upon thee, art not ashamed?

Margaret

Of what, lady? Of speaking honourably? Is not marriage honourable in a beggar? Is not your lord

29 *honourable*: 'holy Matrimony . . . is an honourable estate' ('Order for the Solemnization of Matrimony' in *The Book of Common Prayer*).

30 *saving your reverence*: if you don't mind me saying so.

30–1 *An . . . speaking*: i.e. 'if your dirty mind doesn't twist my words'.

34 *light*: wanton, promiscuous.

36 *coz*: a term of endearment (= cousin).

38 *sick*: sad.

40 *Clap 's . . . love'*: let's sing a round of 'Light o' love'—a popular song (the words are unknown) whose rhythm could be started by clapping.

41 *burden*: bass part for male voices.

42 *light o' love*: wanton, promiscuous.

44 *barns*: bairns (= babies).

45 *illegitimate construction*: false interpretation (with obvious double meaning).

45–6 *with my heels*: by kicking backwards (like a horse).

49 *Heigh-ho*: Beatrice sighs.

51 *h*: ache (then, like the letter, pronounced 'aitch').

52 *an*: if.
turned Turk: changed faith; the phrase was proverbial.

53 *the star*: i.e. the Pole Star, navigational fixed point.

54 *trow*: do you know, I wonder.

55–6 *God . . . desire*: 'Delight thou in the Lord: and he shall give thee thy heart's desire' (Psalm 37:4 in the *Book of Common Prayer*).

---

30 honourable without marriage? I think you would have me say 'saving your reverence, a husband'. An bad thinking do not wrest true speaking, I'll offend nobody. Is there any harm in 'the heavier for a husband'? None, I think, an it be the right husband and the right wife; otherwise 'tis light and not heavy.

35 Ask my Lady Beatrice else. Here she comes.

Enter Beatrice

Hero
Good morrow, coz.
Beatrice
Good morrow, sweet Hero.
Hero
Why, how now? Do you speak in the sick tune?
Beatrice
I am out of all other tune, methinks.
Margaret
40 Clap 's into 'Light o' love'; that goes without a burden. Do you sing it, and I'll dance it.
Beatrice
Ye light o' love with your heels! Then if your husband have stables enough, you'll see he shall lack no barns.
Margaret
45 O illegitimate construction! I scorn that with my heels.
Beatrice
[*To* Hero] 'Tis almost five o'clock, cousin. 'Tis time you were ready. By my troth, I am exceeding ill. Heigh-ho!
Margaret
50 For a hawk, a horse, or a husband?
Beatrice
For the letter that begins them all—h.
Margaret
Well, an you be not turned Turk, there's no more sailing by the star.
Beatrice
What means the fool, trow?
Margaret
55 Nothing, I. But God send everyone their heart's desire.

57 *are*: have.
58 *perfume*: Gloves were usually perfumed to disguise the smell of the leather.

59 *am stuffed*: have a cold in the head—but Margaret is quick to hear innuendo.

63 *professed apprehension*: prided yourself on your wit.

65 *rarely*: splendidly; Beatrice understands 'infrequently'.

66 *in your cap*: i.e. as a fool wears a coxcomb.

68 *carduus benedictus*: 'holy thistle', a popular remedy for all ailments.
69 *qualm*: sudden nausea.

70 *prick'st . . . thistle*: Hero seems to have joined in with the other girls' bawdy jokes.

73–85 *Moral . . . do*: Margaret talks nonsense to divert Beatrice's suspicion.
74 *plain*: simply, literally.
75 *by'r Lady*: by Our Lady (the Virgin Mary).
76 *list*: please.

82–3 *in despite . . . grudging*: 'even though he's in love, he doesn't make such a fuss about it'.

86 *What . . . keeps*: whatever are you trying to say.
87 *Not . . . gallop*: nothing that's not true; a 'false gallop' was only a rapid canter.

Hero
These gloves the count sent me, they are an excellent perfume.

Beatrice
I am stuffed, cousin; I cannot smell.

Margaret
60 A maid, and stuffed! There's goodly catching of cold.

Beatrice
O, God help me, God help me. How long have you professed apprehension?

Margaret
Ever since you left it. Doth not my wit become me
65 rarely?

Beatrice
It is not seen enough. You should wear it in your cap. By my troth, I am sick.

Margaret
Get you some of this distilled *carduus benedictus*, and lay it to your heart. It is the only thing for a qualm.

Hero
70 There thou prick'st her with a thistle.

Beatrice
Benedictus—why *benedictus*? You have some moral in this *benedictus*.

Margaret
Moral? No, by my troth, I have no moral meaning. I meant plain holy-thistle. You may think perchance
75 that I think you are in love. Nay, by'r Lady, I am not such a fool to think what I list. Nor I list not to think what I can, nor indeed I cannot think—if I would think my heart out of thinking—that you are in love, or that you will be in love, or that you can be in love.
80 Yet Benedick was such another, and now is he become a man. He swore he would never marry, and yet now in despite of his heart he eats his meat without grudging. And how you may be converted I know not, but methinks you look with your eyes, as
85 other women do.

Beatrice
What pace is this that thy tongue keeps?

Margaret
Not a false gallop.

Enter Ursula

Ursula
[*To* Hero] Madam, withdraw. The prince, the count,
Signor Benedick, Don John, and all the gallants of
90 the town are come to fetch you to church.
Hero
Help to dress me, good coz, good Meg, good Ursula.
[*Exeunt*

Act 3   Scene 5

Dogberry reports his arrest to Leonato, who
is too busy to listen to him.

2 *confidence*: confidential conference; this
    time Dogberry means what he says.
3 *decerns*: concerns.

Scene 5

Enter Leonato, Dogberry *the constable, and*
Verges *the Headborough*

Leonato
What would you with me, honest neighbour?
Dogberry
Marry, sir, I would have some confidence with you
that decerns you nearly.
Leonato
Brief, I pray you, for you see it is a busy time with
5 me.

Dogberry
Marry, this it is, sir.

Verges
Yes, in truth it is, sir.

Leonato
What is it, my good friends?

Dogberry
Goodman Verges, sir, speaks a little off the matter—
10 an old man, sir, and his wits are not so blunt as, God
help, I would desire they were. But in faith, honest as
the skin between his brows.

Verges
Yes, I thank God, I am as honest as any man living
that is an old man and no honester than I.

Dogberry
15 Comparisons are odorous. '*Palabras*', neighbour
Verges.

Leonato
Neighbours, you are tedious.

Dogberry
It pleases your worship to say so, but we are the poor
duke's officers. But truly, for mine own part, if I were
20 as tedious as a king I could find in my heart to
bestow it all of your worship.

Leonato
All thy tediousness on me, ah?

Dogberry
Yea, an 'twere a thousand pound more than 'tis, for
I hear as good exclamation on your worship as of any
25 man in the city, and though I be but a poor man, I
am glad to hear it.

Verges
And so am I.

Leonato
I would fain know what you have to say.

Verges
Marry, sir, our watch tonight, excepting your
30 worship's presence, ha' ta'en a couple of as arrant
knaves as any in Messina.

Dogberry
A good old man, sir. He will be talking. As they say,
when the age is in, the wit is out. God help us, it is a
world to see. Well said, i' faith, neighbour Verges.

11–12 *honest . . . brows*: The expression was proverbial.

15 *odorous*: i.e. 'odious'.
Palabras: The Spanish expression '*pocas palabras*' (= few words) was popular at this time.

17 *tedious*: Dogberry takes this for flattery (perhaps meaning 'generous').

24 *exclamation*: i.e. 'acclamation'.

33 *when . . . out*: Dogberry garbles the proverb 'When *ale* is in, wit is out'.

35 Well, God's a good man. An two men ride of a horse, one must ride behind. An honest soul, i' faith, sir, by my troth he is, as ever broke bread. But God is to be worshipped; all men are not alike, alas, good neighbour.

Leonato

40 Indeed, neighbour, he comes too short of you.

Dogberry

Gifts that God gives!

Leonato

I must leave you.

Dogberry

One word, sir. Our watch, sir, have indeed comprehended two auspicious persons, and we
45 would have them this morning examined before your worship.

Leonato

Take their examination yourself, and bring it me. I am now in great haste, as it may appear unto you.

Dogberry

It shall be suffigance.

Leonato

50 Drink some wine ere you go. Fare you well.

Enter a Messenger

Messenger

My lord, they stay for you to give your daughter to her husband.

Leonato

I'll wait upon them, I am ready.

[*Exeunt* Leonato *and* Messenger

Dogberry

Go, good partner, go get you to Francis Seacoal. Bid
55 him bring his pen and inkhorn to the jail. We are now to examination these men.

Verges

And we must do it wisely.

Dogberry

We will spare for no wit, I warrant you. Here's that shall drive some of them to a non-com. Only get the
60 learned writer to set down our excommunication, and meet me at the jail. [*Exeunt*

---

40 *comes . . . you*: isn't your equal.

44 *comprehended*: i.e. 'apprehended'.
auspicious: i.e. 'suspicious'.

49 *suffigance*: sufficient.

58 *that*: Dogberry indicates his head.

59 *non-com*: Perhaps Dogberry intends 'nonplus' (= bafflement, perplexity) but in fact his expression suggests '*non compos mentis*' (= out of their minds).

Act 4

Act 4   Scene 1

The wedding party assembles and Claudio denounces Hero—who faints with the shock. The friar has a scheme to make all well, and Benedick offers his services to Beatrice with his love—which she accepts and returns.

1–2 *plain form*: simple formalities (without lengthy sermonizing).

11–13 *If either . . . utter it*: 'if either of you know any impediment, why you may not be lawfully joined together in Matrimony, you do now confess it' ('Order for the Solemnization of Matrimony' in *The Book of Common Prayer*).

11 *inward*: secret.

Scene 1

Enter Don Pedro *the prince*, Don John *the bastard*, Leonato, Friar Francis, Claudio, Benedick, Hero, *and* Beatrice, *with* Guests *and* Attendants

Leonato
Come, Friar Francis, be brief. Only to the plain form of marriage, and you shall recount their particular duties afterwards.

Friar
[*To* Claudio] You come hither, my lord, to marry this
5 lady?

Claudio
No.

Leonato
To be married to her. Friar, you come to marry her.

Friar
[*To* Hero] Lady, you come hither to be married to this count?

Hero
10 I do.

Friar
If either of you know any inward impediment why you should not be conjoined, I charge you on your souls to utter it.

Claudio
Know you any, Hero?

Hero
15 None, my lord.

Friar
Know you any, Count?

Leonato

I dare make his answer—none.

Claudio

O, what men dare do! What men may do! What men daily do, not knowing what they do!

Benedick

20 How now! Interjections? Why then, some be of laughing, as 'ah, ha, he!'

Claudio

Stand thee by, Friar. [*To* Leonato] Father, by your leave,

Will you with free and unconstrained soul

Give me this maid, your daughter?

Leonato

25 As freely, son, as God did give her me.

Claudio

And what have I to give you back whose worth

May counterpoise this rich and precious gift?

Don Pedro

Nothing, unless you render her again.

Claudio

Sweet Prince, you learn me noble thankfulness.

30 There, Leonato, take her back again.

Give not this rotten orange to your friend!

She's but the sign and semblance of her honour.

Behold how like a maid she blushes here.

O, what authority and show of truth

35 Can cunning sin cover itself withal!

Comes not that blood as modest evidence

To witness simple virtue? Would you not swear—

All you that see her—that she were a maid,

By these exterior shows? But she is none.

40 She knows the heat of a luxurious bed.

Her blush is guiltiness, not modesty.

Leonato

What do you mean, my lord?

Claudio

                                        Not to be married,

Not to knit my soul to an approved wanton.

Leonato

Dear my lord, if you in your own proof

45 Have vanquish'd the resistance of her youth

And made defeat of her virginity—

20–1 *some . . . he*: Benedick quotes William Lyly's Latin grammar, a standard school text: 'Some [interjections] are of . . . laughing: as *Ha, ha, he.*'

22 *by your leave*: if I may so call you.

23 *unconstrained*: unconstrainèd.

24 *maid*: virgin.

29 *learn*: teach.

37 *witness*: give evidence of.

40 *luxurious*: lustful.

43 *approved*: approvèd; proven.

44 *in . . . proof*: to test it for yourself.

47 *known*: had intercourse with.
48-9 *embrace . . . sin*: The formal
  engagement of *2, 1, 280–2* constitutes a
  legally valid 'marriage by pre-
  contract'—which would permit such
  'forehand' embracing.
51 *word . . . large*: improper suggestions.

55 *Out on*: that's enough of.
  write against: denounce.
56 *Dian . . . orb*: Diana, the chaste goddess
  of the moon.
57 *blown*: fully opened.

59 *Venus*: goddess of desire and sexual love.
  those pamper'd animals: horses (believed
  by the Elizabethans to be sexually over-
  active).
61 *wide*: wide of the mark, inaccurately.
64 *stale*: whore.

73 *kindly power*: power of kinship.

Claudio
I know what you would say. If I have known her,
You will say she did embrace me as a husband,
And so extenuate the forehand sin.
50 No, Leonato,
I never tempted her with word too large,
But as a brother to his sister show'd
Bashful sincerity and comely love.
      Hero
And seem'd I ever otherwise to you?
      Claudio
55 Out on thy seeming! I will write against it.
You seem to me as Dian in her orb,
As chaste as is the bud ere it be blown.
But you are more intemperate in your blood
Than Venus or those pamper'd animals
60 That rage in savage sensuality.
      Hero
Is my lord well that he doth speak so wide?
      Leonato
Sweet Prince, why speak not you?
      Don Pedro
                              What should I speak?
I stand dishonour'd, that have gone about
To link my dear friend to a common stale.
      Leonato
65 Are these things spoken, or do I but dream?
      Don John
Sir, they are spoken, and these things are true.
      Benedick
This looks not like a nuptial.
      Hero
                              True? O God!
      Claudio
Leonato, stand I here?
Is this the prince? Is this the prince's brother?
70 Is this face Hero's? Are our eyes our own?
      Leonato
All this is so. But what of this, my lord?
      Claudio
Let me but move one question to your daughter,
And by that fatherly and kindly power
That you have in her, bid her answer truly.

77 *catechizing*: Elizabethan children were taught their religion by a question-and-answer catechism which began 'What is your name?'

78 *answer . . . name*: acknowledge that you are what we have called you (i.e. unchaste).

Leonato

75 [*To* Hero] I charge thee do so, as thou art my child.

Hero

O God defend me! How am I beset!
What kind of catechizing call you this?

Claudio

To make you answer truly to your name.

Hero

Is it not Hero? Who can blot that name

80 With any just reproach?

Claudio

                                        Marry, that can Hero.
Hero itself can blot out Hero's virtue.
What man was he talk'd with you yesternight
Out at your window betwixt twelve and one?
Now, if you are a maid, answer to this.

Hero

85 I talk'd with no man at that hour, my lord.

Don Pedro

Why, then are you no maiden. Leonato,
I am sorry you must hear. Upon mine honour,
Myself, my brother, and this grieved count
Did see her, hear her, at that hour last night

90 Talk with a ruffian at her chamber window,
Who hath indeed, most like a liberal villain,
Confess'd the vile encounters they have had
A thousand times in secret.

Don John

                                        Fie, fie, they are
Not to be nam'd, my lord, not to be spoke of.

95 There is not chastity enough in language
Without offence to utter them. Thus, pretty lady,
I am sorry for thy much misgovernment.

Claudio

O Hero! What a Hero hadst thou been
If half thy outward graces had been plac'd

100 About thy thoughts and counsels of thy heart!
But fare thee well, most foul, most fair; farewell
Thou pure impiety and impious purity.
For thee I'll lock up all the gates of love,
And on my eyelids shall conjecture hang

105 To turn all beauty into thoughts of harm,
And never shall it more be gracious.

88 *grieved*: grievèd; wronged.

91 *liberal*: licentious.

97 *misgovernment*: misconduct.

103 *gates of love*: the senses (especially the eyes).
104 *conjecture*: suspicion.

Leonato
Hath no man's dagger here a point for me?

Hero falls to the ground

Beatrice
Why, how now, cousin, wherefore sink you down?
Don John
Come, let us go. These things come thus to light
110 Smother her spirits up.
           [*Exeunt* Don Pedro, Don John, *and* Claudio
Benedick
How doth the lady?
Beatrice
           Dead, I think. Help, uncle.
Hero, why Hero! Uncle, Signor Benedick, Friar—
Leonato
O Fate, take not away thy heavy hand.
Death is the fairest cover for her shame
115 That may be wish'd for.
Beatrice
            How now, cousin Hero?
Friar
Have comfort, lady.
Leonato
Dost thou look up?
Friar
Yea, wherefore should she not?
Leonato
Wherefore? Why, doth not every earthly thing
120 Cry shame upon her? Could she here deny
The story that is printed in her blood?
Do not live, Hero, do not ope thine eyes;
For did I think thou wouldst not quickly die,
Thought I thy spirits were stronger than thy shames,
125 Myself would, on the rearward of reproaches,
Strike at thy life. Griev'd I, I had but one?
Chid I for that at frugal nature's frame?
O one too much by thee! Why had I one?
Why ever wast thou lovely in my eyes?
130 Why had I not with charitable hand
Took up a beggar's issue at my gates,
Who, smirched thus, and mir'd with infamy,
I might have said 'No part of it is mine;

110 *spirits*: the vital powers controlling bodily functions.

117 *look up*: i.e. to heaven (imploring aid).

121 *printed . . . blood*: shown in her blushes of shame, stamped on her life.

125 *on the rearward of*: immediately after.

127 *frame*: plan.

131 *issue*: child.
132 *smirched*: smirchèd.

135–7 *mine . . . mine*: i.e. 'I cared so much for my child that I took no care of myself.'

141 *salt . . . season*: The Elizabethans used salt to preserve their meat.

146 *bedfellow*: It was usual in Elizabethan days for two adults of the same sex to share a bed.

153 *tears*: Claudio perhaps shed tears of disappointed rage when he accused Hero.
159 *shames*: embarrassments.
163 *maiden truth*: the truth of her virginity.
165 *experimental seal*: validation of experience.
165–6 *warrant . . . book*: confirm the substance of my reading.

This shame derives itself from unknown loins.'
135 But mine, and mine I lov'd, and mine I prais'd,
And mine that I was proud on; mine so much
That I myself was to myself not mine,
Valuing of her—why she, O she is fallen
Into a pit of ink, that the wide sea
140 Hath drops too few to wash her clean again,
And salt too little which may season give
To her foul, tainted flesh.
  Benedick
       Sir, sir, be patient.
For my part, I am so attir'd in wonder
I know not what to say.
  Beatrice
145 O, on my soul, my cousin is belied.
  Benedick
Lady, were you her bedfellow last night?
  Beatrice
No, truly not, although until last night
I have this twelvemonth been her bedfellow.
  Leonato
Confirm'd, confirm'd. O, that is stronger made
150 Which was before barr'd up with ribs of iron.
Would the two princes lie? And Claudio lie,
Who lov'd her so that, speaking of her foulness,
Wash'd it with tears? Hence from her, let her die.
  Friar
Hear me a little,
155 For I have only silent been so long
And given way unto this course of fortune.
By noting of the lady, I have mark'd
A thousand blushing apparitions
To start into her face, a thousand innocent shames
160 In angel whiteness beat away those blushes,
And in her eye there hath appear'd a fire
To burn the errors that these princes hold
Against her maiden truth. Call me a fool,
Trust not my reading nor my observations,
165 Which with experimental seal doth warrant
The tenor of my book. Trust not my age,
My reverence, calling, nor divinity,
If this sweet lady lie not guiltless here
Under some biting error.

Leonato

Friar, it cannot be.

170 Thou seest that all the grace that she hath left
Is that she will not add to her damnation
A sin of perjury. She not denies it.
Why seek'st thou then to cover with excuse

174 *proper*: natural, undisguised.

That which appears in proper nakedness?

Friar

175 Lady, what man is he you are accus'd of?

Hero

They know that do accuse me; I know none.
If I know more of any man alive
Than that which maiden modesty doth warrant,
Let all my sins lack mercy. O my father,

180 Prove you that any man with me convers'd

181 *unmeet*: improper.

At hours unmeet, or that I yesternight
Maintain'd the change of words with any creature,
Refuse me, hate me, torture me to death.

Friar

184 *misprision*: misunderstanding.

There is some strange misprision in the princes.

Benedick

185 *the very bent of*: the right inclination to.

185 Two of them have the very bent of honour,
And if their wisdoms be misled in this

187 *practice*: trickery.
   John the Bastard: This is the first time
   any of the characters has given this
   description.
188 *frame*: designing.

The practice of it lives in John the Bastard,
Whose spirits toil in frame of villainies.

Leonato

I know not. If they speak but truth of her,

190 These hands shall tear her. If they wrong her
   honour,
The proudest of them shall well hear of it.
Time hath not yet so dried this blood of mine,
Nor age so eat up my invention,

193 *invention*: resourcefulness. The word
   here is pronounced with four syllables.

Nor fortune made such havoc of my means,

195 *reft*: bereft.

195 Nor my bad life reft me so much of friends,
But they shall find awak'd in such a kind
Both strength of limb and policy of mind,

197 *policy*: ingenuity.

Ability in means, and choice of friends,

199 *quit . . . throughly*: pay them back in
   full.

To quit me of them throughly.

Friar

Pause a while,

200 And let my counsel sway you in this case.
Your daughter here the princes left for dead.

202 *in*: at home.	Let her a while be secretly kept in,
	And publish it that she is dead indeed.
204 *mourning ostentation*: show of mourning.	Maintain a mourning ostentation,
205 *monument*: burial vault.	205 And on your family's old monument
	Hang mournful epitaphs, and do all rites
	That appertain unto a burial.

Leonato
What shall become of this? What will this do?
Friar
Marry, this, well carried, shall on her behalf
210 Change slander to remorse. That is some good.
But not for that dream I on this strange course,
But on this travail look for greater birth.
She dying—as it must be so maintain'd—
Upon the instant that she was accus'd,
215 Shall be lamented, pitied, and excus'd
Of every hearer. For it so falls out
That what we have we prize not to the worth
Whiles we enjoy it, but being lack'd and lost,
Why, then we rack the value, then we find
220 The virtue that possession would not show us
Whiles it was ours. So will it fare with Claudio.
When he shall hear she died upon his words,
Th'idea of her life shall sweetly creep
Into his study of imagination,
225 And every lovely organ of her life
Shall come apparell'd in more precious habit,
More moving, delicate, and full of life,
Into the eye and prospect of his soul
Than when she liv'd indeed. Then shall he mourn,
230 If ever love had interest in his liver,
And wish he had not so accused her—
No, though he thought his accusation true.
Let this be so, and doubt not but success
Will fashion the event in better shape
235 Than I can lay it down in likelihood.
But if all aim but this be levell'd false,
The supposition of the lady's death
Will quench the wonder of her infamy.
And if it sort not well, you may conceal her,
240 As best befits her wounded reputation,
In some reclusive and religious life,

Marginal glosses:

212 *travail*: labour.

216 *Of*: by.
217 *not . . . worth*: as much as it is worth.

219 *rack*: stretch out, exaggerate.

224 *his . . . imagination*: his pensive thoughts.
225 *organ*: aspect.
226 *habit*: attire.
227 *moving*: affecting.

230 *had interest in*: had any part of.
liver: This was thought to be the seat of love.
231 *accused*: accusèd.
233 *success*: succeeding events.
234 *event*: outcome.

236 *if . . . false*: if we miss our aim in every other respect but this.

238 *wonder*: gossip.
239 *sort*: turn out.

241 *reclusive*: cloistered.

Out of all eyes, tongues, minds, and injuries.

Benedick

Signor Leonato, let the friar advise you;

244 *inwardness*: intimate friendship.

And though you know my inwardness and love

245 Is very much unto the prince and Claudio,

Yet, by mine honour, I will deal in this

As secretly and justly as your soul

Should with your body.

Leonato

248 *flow in grief*: am overwhelmed by grief.

249 *twine*: thread.

                                      Being that I flow in grief,

The smallest twine may lead me.

Friar

250 'Tis well consented. Presently away,

251 *to strange . . . cure*: A proverbial saying: desperate diseases must have desperate cures.

253 *Perhaps . . . endure*: A line of 12 syllables (alexandrine) brings the episode to its close.

prolong'd: postponed.

For to strange sores strangely they strain the cure.

[*To* Hero] Come, lady, die to live. This wedding day

Perhaps is but prolong'd. Have patience and endure.

                         [*Exeunt all but* Beatrice *and* Benedick

Benedick

Lady Beatrice, have you wept all this while?

Beatrice

255 Yea, and I will weep a while longer.

Benedick

I will not desire that.

Beatrice

You have no reason; I do it freely.

Benedick

Surely I do believe your fair cousin is wronged.

Beatrice

Ah, how much might the man deserve of me that

260 would right her!

Benedick

Is there any way to show such friendship?

Beatrice

262 *even*: direct.

A very even way, but no such friend.

Benedick

May a man do it?

Beatrice

It is a man's office, but not yours.

264 *office*: task.

Benedick

265 I do love nothing in the world so well as you. Is not

that strange?

267 *the thing I know not*: I don't know what.
272 *By my sword*: The oath of a Christian gentleman, sworn on the cross made by the hilt of his weapon.

273 *eat it*: eat the sword—i.e. his words.
277 *protest*: declare.
279 *God forgive me*: i.e. for being about to flout convention and be the first to declare her love.

281 *stayed*: stopped, forestalled.
     in a happy hour: at a propitious moment.

291 *I am gone . . . here*: 'I have gone in spirit, though I am held here by force.'

Beatrice
As strange as the thing I know not. It were as possible for me to say I loved nothing so well as you. But believe me not, and yet I lie not. I confess 270 nothing nor I deny nothing; I am sorry for my cousin.
Benedick
By my sword, Beatrice, thou lovest me.
Beatrice
Do not swear and eat it.
Benedick
I will swear by it that you love me, and I will make 275 him eat it that says I love not you.
Beatrice
Will you not eat your word?
Benedick
With no sauce that can be devised to it. I protest I love thee.
Beatrice
Why then, God forgive me.
Benedick
280 What offence, sweet Beatrice?
Beatrice
You have stayed me in a happy hour. I was about to protest I loved you.
Benedick
And do it with all thy heart.
Beatrice
I love you with so much of my heart that none is left 285 to protest.
Benedick
Come, bid me do anything for thee.
Beatrice
Kill Claudio.
Benedick
Ha! Not for the wide world.
Beatrice
You kill me to deny it. Farewell.
Benedick
290 [*Barring her way*] Tarry, sweet Beatrice.
Beatrice
I am gone though I am here. There is no love in you.—Nay, I pray you, let me go.

Benedick

Beatrice—

Beatrice

In faith, I will go.

Benedick

295 We'll be friends first.

Beatrice

You dare easier be friends with me than fight with mine enemy.

Benedick

Is Claudio thine enemy?

Beatrice

Is a not approved in the height a villain, that hath 300 slandered, scorned, dishonoured my kinswoman? O that I were a man! What, bear her in hand until they come to take hands, and then with public accusation, uncovered slander, unmitigated rancour—O God that I were a man! I would eat his 305 heart in the market place.

Benedick

Hear me, Beatrice—

Beatrice

Talk with a man out at a window—a proper saying!

Benedick

Nay, but Beatrice—

Beatrice

Sweet Hero! She is wronged, she is slandered, she is 310 undone.

Benedick

Beat—

Beatrice

Princes and counties! Surely a princely testimony, a goodly count; Count Comfit, a sweet gallant, surely. O that I were a man for his sake! Or that I had any 315 friend would be a man for my sake! But manhood is melted into curtsies, valour into compliment, and men are only turned into tongue, and trim ones, too. He is now as valiant as Hercules that only tells a lie and swears it. I cannot be a man with wishing; 320 therefore I will die a woman with grieving.

Benedick

Tarry, good Beatrice. By this hand, I love thee.

301 *bear . . . hand*: lead her on with false pretences.
302 *take hands*: join hands in marriage.
303 *uncovered*: bare-faced.

307 *proper saying*: likely story.

313 *count*: Beatrice makes a triple pun on 'count' (= Claudio, = account/narrative, = legal indictment).
Count Comfit: Count Candy.
316 *curtsies*: courtesies, ceremonies.
compliment: flattery.
317 *only . . . tongue*: become all talk.
trim: smooth.
318 *Hercules*: the superman of classical mythology.

Beatrice

Use it for my love some other way than swearing by it.

Benedick

Think you in your soul the Count Claudio hath wronged Hero?

Beatrice

325 Yea, as sure as I have a thought or a soul.

Benedick

Enough, I am engaged; I will challenge him. I will kiss your hand, and so I leave you. By this hand, Claudio shall render me a dear account. As you hear of me, so think of me. Go comfort your cousin. I

330 must say she is dead. And so, farewell.

[*Exeunt*

Act 4   Scene 2

Dogberry and Verges examine their prisoners.

os.d. *gowns*: i.e. the official black gowns appropriate to their offices.

2 *stool . . . cushion*: i.e. so that he can sit and write notes.

5–6 *exhibition to examine*: commission to conduct an examination.

Scene 2

Enter Dogberry, Verges, *and the* Sexton *in gowns*; *and the* Watch, *with* Conrad *and* Borachio

Dogberry

Is our whole dissembly appeared?

Verges

O, a stool and a cushion for the sexton.

Sexton

[*Sits*] Which be the malefactors?

Dogberry

Marry, that am I, and my partner.

Verges

5 Nay, that's certain; we have the exhibition to examine.

Sexton

But which are the offenders that are to be examined? Let them come before Master Constable.

Dogberry

Yea, marry, let them come before me. What is your

10 name, friend?

Borachio

Borachio.

Dogberry

[*To the* Sexton] Pray write down 'Borachio'. [*To* Conrad] Yours, sirrah?

13 *sirrah*: A contemptuous form of 'sir', used to address social inferiors.

Conrad

I am a gentleman, sir, and my name is Conrad.

Dogberry

15 Write down 'Master Gentleman Conrad'. Masters, do you serve God?

Conrad and **Borachio**

Yea, sir, we hope.

Dogberry

Write down that they hope they serve God. And write 'God' first, for God defend but God should go

19 *defend*: forbid.

20 before such villains. Masters, it is proved already that you are little better than false knaves, and it will go near to be thought so shortly. How answer you for yourselves?

Conrad

Marry, sir, we say we are none.

Dogberry

25–6 *go about with*: get the better of.

25 A marvellous witty fellow, I assure you, but I will go about with him.—Come you hither, sirrah. A word in your ear, sir. I say to you it is thought you are false knaves.

Borachio

Sir, I say to you we are none.

Dogberry

30 Well, stand aside. Fore God, they are both in a tale. Have you writ down that they are none?

Sexton

Master Constable, you go not the way to examine. You must call forth the watch that are their accusers.

Dogberry

34 *eftest*: quickest.

Yea, marry, that's the eftest way. Let the watch come

35 forth.—Masters, I charge you in the prince's name accuse these men.

A Watchman

This man said, sir, that Don John, the prince's brother, was a villain.

Dogberry

Write down Prince John a villain. Why, this is flat

40 perjury, to call a prince's brother villain.

Borachio
Master Constable—
    Dogberry
Pray thee, fellow, peace. I do not like thy look, I
promise thee.
    Sexton
What heard you him say else?
    A Watchman
45 Marry, that he had received a thousand ducats of
Don John for accusing the Lady Hero wrongfully.
    Dogberry
Flat burglary, as ever was committed.
    Verges
Yea, by th'mass, that it is.
    Sexton
What else, fellow?
    A Watchman
50 And that Count Claudio did mean upon his words to
disgrace Hero before the whole assembly, and not
marry her.
    Dogberry
O villain! Thou wilt be condemned into everlasting
redemption for this.
    Sexton
55 What else?
    A Watchman
This is all.
    Sexton
And this is more, masters, than you can deny. Prince
John is this morning secretly stolen away. Hero was
in this manner accused, in this very manner refused,
60 and upon the grief of this suddenly died. Master
Constable, let these men be bound and brought to
Leonato's. I will go before and show him their
examination.   [*Exit*
    Dogberry
Come, let them be opinioned.
    Verges
65 Let them be in the hands—

         Watchmen *seize* Conrad *and* Borachio

48 *by th' mass*: by the mass.

64 *opinioned*: pinioned, bound.

66 *coxcomb*: fool (the fool's cap was crowned with a crest like that of a cock).

67 *God s' my life*: May God save my life.
69 *naughty*: wicked.
73 *suspect*: i.e. 'respect'.

80 *pretty . . . flesh*: Dogberry is proud of his appearance.
81 *go to*: 'I can tell you', 'believe me'; the phrase is simply an intensifier.
82 *losses*: Even Dogberry's financial disasters give him cause for self-satisfaction.

Conrad
Off, coxcomb!

Dogberry
God s' my life, where's the sexton? Let him write down the prince's officer coxcomb. Come, bind them. [*To* Conrad, *who resists*]—Thou naughty
70 varlet!

Conrad
Away, you are an ass; you are an ass.

Dogberry
Dost thou not suspect my place? Dost thou not suspect my years? O that he were here to write me down an ass! But, masters, remember that I am an
75 ass. Though it be not written down, yet forget not that I am an ass. No, thou villain, thou art full of piety, as shall be proved upon thee by good witness. I am a wise fellow, and which is more, an officer; and which is more, a householder; and which is more, as
80 pretty a piece of flesh as any is in Messina; and one that knows the law, go to; and a rich fellow enough, go to; and a fellow that hath had losses; and one that hath two gowns, and everything handsome about him.—Bring him away. O that I had been writ down
85 an ass! [*Exeunt*

Act 5

Leonato, still grieving, attempts to challenge Claudio. Don Pedro keeps the peace—but Benedick presents a new challenge. Dogberry brings in his prisoners, and Borachio confesses all. Leonato promises a new bride for Claudio.

2 *second*: assist.

7 *suit*: correspond.

12 *answer . . . strain*: respond with like emotions (or musical tones).

16 *wag*: clear off.
   cry 'hem': clear his throat (before drinking).
17 *Patch*: mend, console.
   make . . . drunk: drown his sorrows.
18 *candle-wasters*: late-night drinkers.

22 *not feel*: do not feel.

24 *preceptial medicine*: proverbs as medicine.

27 *office*: business.

Scene 1

Enter Leonato *and* Antonio *his brother*

Antonio
If you go on thus, you will kill yourself,
And 'tis not wisdom thus to second grief
Against yourself.
Leonato
                    I pray thee cease thy counsel,
Which falls into mine ears as profitless
5   As water in a sieve. Give not me counsel,
Nor let no comforter delight mine ear
But such a one whose wrongs do suit with mine.
Bring me a father that so lov'd his child,
Whose joy of her is overwhelm'd like mine,
10 And bid him speak of patience.
Measure his woe the length and breadth of mine,
And let it answer every strain for strain,
As thus for thus, and such a grief for such,
In every lineament, branch, shape, and form.
15 If such a one will smile and stroke his beard,
Bid sorrow wag, cry 'hem' when he should groan,
Patch grief with proverbs, make misfortune drunk
With candle-wasters, bring him yet to me,
And I of him will gather patience.
20 But there is no such man. For, brother, men
Can counsel and speak comfort to that grief
Which they themselves not feel. But tasting it,
Their counsel turns to passion, which before
Would give preceptial medicine to rage,
25 Fetter strong madness in a silken thread,
Charm ache with air and agony with words.
No, no, 'tis all men's office to speak patience

28 *wring*: writhe.
29 *virtue*: power.
   sufficiency: ability.
30 *moral*: righteous.

32 *advertisement*: advice.

33 *Therein . . . differ*: Antonio hints that his brother is being childish.

37 *writ . . . gods*: written with the authority of gods.
38 *made a pish*: scoffed at.

39 *bend*: turn.

49 *all is one*: it doesn't matter.

To those that wring under the load of sorrow,
But no man's virtue nor sufficiency
30 To be so moral when he shall endure
The like himself. Therefore give me no counsel.
My griefs cry louder than advertisement.
        Antonio
Therein do men from children nothing differ.
        Leonato
I pray thee peace. I will be flesh and blood,
35 For there was never yet philosopher
That could endure the toothache patiently,
However they have writ the style of gods,
And made a pish at chance and sufferance.
        Antonio
Yet bend not all the harm upon yourself.
40 Make those that do offend you suffer too.
        Leonato
There thou speak'st reason; nay, I will do so.
My soul doth tell me Hero is belied,
And that shall Claudio know; so shall the prince,
And all of them that thus dishonour her.

        Enter Don Pedro *the prince and* Claudio

        Antonio
45 Here comes the prince and Claudio hastily.
        Don Pedro
Good e'en, good e'en.
        Claudio
                        Good day to both of you.
        Leonato
Hear you, my lords!
        Don Pedro
                        We have some haste, Leonato.
        Leonato
Some haste, my lord! Well, fare you well, my lord.
Are you so hasty now? Well, all is one.
        Don Pedro
50 Nay, do not quarrel with us, good old man.
        Antonio
If he could right himself with quarrelling,
Some of us would lie low.
        Claudio
                        Who wrongs him?

Leonato

Marry,

53 *Thou*: The intimate form is intended as an insult.

Thou dost wrong me, thou dissembler, thou.
Nay, never lay thy hand upon thy sword;
55 I fear thee not.

Claudio

Marry, beshrew my hand

55 *beshrew*: curse.

If it should give your age such cause of fear.
In faith, my hand meant nothing to my sword.

57 *meant nothing*: intended nothing (in moving toward the sword).

Leonato

58 *fleer*: gibe.

Tush, tush, man, never fleer and jest at me.
I speak not like a dotard nor a fool,
60 As under privilege of age to brag
What I have done being young, or what would do

62 *head*: face.
66 *trial of a man*: single combat.

Were I not old. Know, Claudio, to thy head,
Thou hast so wrong'd mine innocent child and me
That I am forc'd to lay my reverence by,
65 And with grey hairs and bruise of many days
Do challenge thee to trial of a man.
I say thou hast belied mine innocent child.
Thy slander hath gone through and through her heart,
And she lies buried with her ancestors—
70 O, in a tomb where never scandal slept
Save this of hers, fram'd by thy villainy.

71 *fram'd*: devised.
75 *nice fence*: fancy swordplay; Leonato scorns the elaborate new fencing techniques popular among the fashionable young men of Shakespeare's day.

Claudio

My villainy?

Leonato

Thine, Claudio, thine I say.

Don Pedro

You say not right, old man.

Leonato

My lord, my lord,
I'll prove it on his body if he dare,
75 Despite his nice fence and his active practice,
His May of youth and bloom of lustihood.

Claudio

Away, I will not have to do with you.

Leonato

78 *doff me*: put me off.
79 *boy*: Leonato uses the final insult.

Canst thou so doff me? Thou hast kill'd my child.
If thou kill'st me, boy, thou shalt kill a man.

Antonio

80 He shall kill two of us, and men indeed.
But that's no matter, let him kill one first.
Win me and wear me. Let him answer me.
Come follow me, boy; come, sir boy, come follow
   me.
Sir boy, I'll whip you from your foining fence.

85 Nay, as I am a gentleman, I will.

Leonato

Brother—

Antonio

Content yourself. God knows, I lov'd my niece,
And she is dead, slander'd to death by villains
That dare as well answer a man in deed

90 As I dare take a serpent by the tongue.
Boys, apes, braggarts, jacks, milksops!

Leonato

                                    Brother Antony—

Antonio

Hold you content. What, man, I know them, yea,
And what they weigh, even to the utmost scruple:
Scambling, outfacing, fashion-monging boys,

95 That lie and cog and flout, deprave and slander,
Go anticly, and show an outward hideousness,
And speak off half a dozen dangerous words,
How they might hurt their enemies, if they durst,
And this is all.

Leonato

100 But brother Antony—

Antonio

                        Come, 'tis no matter.
Do not you meddle, let me deal in this.

Don Pedro

Gentlemen both, we will not wake your patience.
My heart is sorry for your daughter's death,
But on my honour she was charg'd with nothing

105 But what was true and very full of proof.

Leonato

My lord, my lord—

Don Pedro

                    I will not hear you.

82 *Win . . . me*: 'Let him overcome me, and then he can boast' (proverbial).

84 *foining fence*: downward thrust in fencing (here with sexual innuendo).

91 *apes*: mimics.
    jacks: knaves.
94 *Scambling*: scuffling.
    outfacing: insolent, bullying.
    fashion-monging: constantly changing fashions.

95 *cog and flout*: cheat and insult.
    deprave: defame.
96 *Go anticly*: dress weirdly.
    show . . . hideousness: look terrible.

Leonato

No?

Come, brother, away. I will be heard.

Antonio

And shall, or some of us will smart for it.

[*Exeunt* Leonato *and* Antonio

Enter Benedick

Don Pedro

See, see, here comes the man we went to seek.

Claudio

110 Now, signor, what news?

Benedick

[*To* Don Pedro] Good day, my lord.

Don Pedro

Welcome, signor. You are almost come to part almost a fray.

Claudio

We had liked to have had our two noses snapped off
115 with two old men without teeth.

Don Pedro

Leonato and his brother. What thinkest thou? Had
we fought, I doubt we should have been too young
for them.

Benedick

In a false quarrel there is no true valour. I came to
120 seek you both.

Claudio

We have been up and down to seek thee, for we are
high-proof melancholy and would fain have it beaten
away. Wilt thou use thy wit?

Benedick

It is in my scabbard. Shall I draw it?

Don Pedro

125 Dost thou wear thy wit by thy side?

Claudio

Never any did so, though very many have been
beside their wit. I will bid thee draw as we do the
minstrels; draw to pleasure us.

Don Pedro

As I am an honest man, he looks pale. Art thou sick,
130 or angry?

114   *had liked*: were likely.
115   *with*: by.

117   *doubt*: fear.

122   *high-proof*: in the highest degree of.

131 *care . . . cat*: A proverbial warning
against too much worry.

133 *in the career*: in mid-gallop (as in
jousting).
an: if.

135 *staff*: lance.
135–6 *broke cross*: snapped across the middle
(because not aimed for a direct strike
against the opponent).

139 *turn his girdle*: what he can do about it;
the expression is proverbial.

143 *make it good*: back up what I say.

144 *Do me right*: accept my challenge.
protest: proclaim.

147–8 *so . . . cheer*: so long as I am well
entertained.

150 *calf's head*: fool.
151 *capon*: coward (a castrated cockerel).
152 *curiously*: skilfully.
naught: rubbish.
153 *woodcock*: idiot (the bird was proverbially
gullible).
154 *ambles well*: goes along very slowly.

155 *wit*: understanding—but the sense
probably develops with sexual innuendo.

Claudio
What, courage, man! What though care killed a cat,
thou hast mettle enough in thee to kill care.

Benedick
Sir, I shall meet your wit in the career, an you charge
it against me. I pray you choose another subject.

Claudio
135 Nay then, give him another staff. This last was broke
cross.

Don Pedro
By this light, he changes more and more. I think he
be angry indeed.

Claudio
If he be, he knows how to turn his girdle.

Benedick
140 Shall I speak a word in your ear?

Claudio
God bless me from a challenge.

Benedick
[*Aside to* Claudio] You are a villain. I jest not. I will
make it good how you dare, with what you dare, and
when you dare. Do me right, or I will protest your
145 cowardice. You have killed a sweet lady, and her
death shall fall heavy on you. Let me hear from you.

Claudio
[*Aside to* Benedick] Well, I will meet you, so I may
have good cheer.

Don Pedro
What, a feast, a feast?

Claudio
150 I' faith, I thank him. He hath bid me to a calf's head
and a capon, the which if I do not carve most
curiously, say my knife's naught. Shall I not find a
woodcock too?

Benedick
Sir, your wit ambles well; it goes easily.

Don Pedro
155 I'll tell thee how Beatrice praised thy wit the other
day. I said thou hadst a fine wit. 'True,' said she, 'a
fine little one.' 'No,' said I, 'a great wit.' 'Right,' says
she, 'a great gross one.' 'Nay,' said I, 'a good wit.'
'Just,' said she, 'it hurts nobody.' 'Nay,' said I, 'the

161 *hath the tongues*: speaks foreign languages.

167 *properest*: finest, most handsome.

170 *an if*: if indeed.

172 *daughter*: Don Pedro (or perhaps the dramatist) has forgotten that Hero is dead.

173–4 *God . . . garden*: Adam was trying, unsuccessfully, to hide himself from God (Genesis 3:8).

175–6 *savage . . . head*: Don Pedro seems unaware that the happy jokes of *Act 1*, Scene 1 are no longer appropriate.

180 *gossip-like humour*: chattering like old women (gossips = godparents).

160 gentleman is wise.' 'Certain,' said she, 'a wise gentleman.' 'Nay,' said I, 'he hath the tongues.' 'That I believe,' said she, 'for he swore a thing to me on Monday night which he forswore on Tuesday morning. There's a double tongue; there's two
165 tongues.' Thus did she an hour together trans-shape thy particular virtues. Yet at last she concluded with a sigh thou wast the properest man in Italy.

Claudio

For the which she wept heartily and said she cared not.

Don Pedro

170 Yea, that she did. But yet for all that, an if she did not hate him deadly, she would love him dearly. The old man's daughter told us all.

Claudio

All, all. And moreover, God saw him when he was hid in the garden.

Don Pedro

175 But when shall we set the savage bull's horns on the sensible Benedick's head?

Claudio

Yea, and text underneath, 'Here dwells Benedick the married man'.

Benedick

[*To* Claudio] Fare you well, boy, you know my mind.
180 I will leave you now to your gossip-like humour. You break jests as braggarts do their blades which, God be thanked, hurt not. [*To* Don Pedro] My lord, for your many courtesies I thank you. I must discontinue your company. Your brother the bastard
185 is fled from Messina. You have among you killed a sweet and innocent lady. For my Lord Lackbeard there, he and I shall meet; and till then, peace be with him.   [*Exit*

Don Pedro

He is in earnest.

Claudio

190 In most profound earnest and, I'll warrant you, for the love of Beatrice.

Don Pedro

And hath challenged thee?

194 *goes*: goes out wearing.

196–7 *He is . . . man*: a fool may then think
        such a man a hero, but then, compared
        to such a man, a fool is a scholar.
197 *doctor*: learned man, scholar.
198–9 *Pluck . . . sad*: pull yourself together
        and be serious.

201 *reasons*: The word was pronounced
        'raisins'—allowing Dogberry an easy
        pun.
202 *cursing*: accursed.
206 *Hearken after*: enquire about.

217 *in . . . division*: with the argument
        properly set out.
218 *one . . . suited*: Between them, Dogberry
        and Don Pedro have presented one idea
        in six ways.

Claudio
Most sincerely.
Don Pedro
What a pretty thing man is when he goes in his
195 doublet and hose and leaves off his wit!

> *Enter* Dogberry *and* Verges, *the* Watch,
> Conrad, *and* Borachio

Claudio
He is then a giant to an ape. But then is an ape a
doctor to such a man.
Don Pedro
But soft you, let me be. Pluck up, my heart, and be
sad. Did he not say my brother was fled? *fliehen*
Dogberry
200 [*To a prisoner*] Come you, sir. If justice cannot tame
you, she shall ne'er weigh more reasons in her
balance. Nay, an you be a cursing hypocrite once,
you must be looked to.
Don Pedro
How now, two of my brother's men bound? Borachio
205 one!
Claudio   *Vergehen*
Hearken after their offence, my lord.
Don Pedro
Officers, what offence have these men done?
Dogberry
Marry, sir, they have committed false report.
Moreover they have spoken untruths; secondarily
210 they are slanders; sixth and lastly they have belied a
lady; thirdly they have verified unjust things and, to
conclude, they are lying knaves. *Spitzbuben*
Don Pedro
First I ask thee what they have done; thirdly I ask
thee what's their offence; sixth and lastly why they
215 are committed and, to conclude, what you lay to
their charge. *Anklage*
Claudio
Rightly reasoned and in his own division. And by my
troth there's one meaning well suited.
Treue **Don Pedro**
[*To* Conrad *and* Borachio] Who have you offended,
220 masters, that you are thus bound to your answer?

221 *cunning*: ingenious.

This learned constable is too cunning to be understood. What's your offence?

Borachio
Sweet Prince, let me go no farther to mine answer. Do you hear me, and let this count kill me. I have
225 deceived even your very eyes. What your wisdoms could not discover, these shallow fools have brought to light, who in the night overheard me confessing to this man how Don John your brother incensed me to slander the Lady Hero, how you were brought into

230–1 *in Hero's garments*: This detail has not been mentioned before.

230 the orchard and saw me court Margaret in Hero's garments, how you disgraced her when you should marry her. My villainy they have upon record, which I had rather seal with my death than repeat over to my shame. The lady is dead upon mine and my
235 master's false accusation; and, briefly, I desire nothing but the reward of a villain.

Don Pedro
[*To* Claudio] Runs not this speech like iron through your blood?

Claudio
I have drunk poison whiles he uttered it.

Don Pedro   außern
240 [*To* Borachio] But did my brother set thee on to this?

Borachio
Yea, and paid me richly for the practice of it.

241 *practice*: performance.

Don Pedro   betrügerisch
He is compos'd and fram'd of treachery, Verrat
And fled he is upon this villainy.

Claudio
Sweet Hero, now thy image doth appear

245 *rare semblance*: wonderful likeness.

245 In the rare semblance that I lov'd it first.

Dogberry   Kläger
Come, bring away the plaintiffs. By this time our sexton hath reformed Signor Leonato of the matter. And, masters, do not forget to specify, when time and place shall serve, that I am an ass.

Verges
250 Here, here comes Master Signor Leonato, and the sexton too.

Enter Leonato, Antonio *his brother, and the*
Sexton

Leonato
Which is the villain? Let me see his eyes,
That when I note another man like him
I may avoid him. Which of these is he?
Borachio
255 If you would know your wronger, look on me.
Leonato
Art thou the slave that with thy breath hast kill'd
Mine innocent child?
Borachio
                              Yea, even I alone.
Leonato
No, not so, villain, thou beliest thyself.
Here stand a pair of honourable men.
260 A third is fled that had a hand in it.
I thank you, princes, for my daughter's death.
Record it with your high and ~~worthy~~ deeds.
'Twas bravely done, if you bethink you of it.
Claudio
I know not how to pray your patience,
265 Yet I must speak. Choose your revenge yourself;
Impose me to what penance your invention
Can lay upon my sin. Yet sinn'd I not
But in mistaking.
Don Pedro
                          By my soul, nor I.
And yet to satisfy this good old man
270 I would bend under any heavy weight
That he'll enjoin me to.
Leonato
I cannot bid you bid my daughter live;
That were impossible; but, I pray you both,
Possess the people in Messina here
275 How innocent she died. And if your love
Can labour aught in sad invention,
Hang her an epitaph upon her tomb
And sing it to her bones; sing it tonight.
Tomorrow morning come you to my house,
280 And since you could not be my son-in-law,
Be yet my nephew. My brother hath a daughter,

264 *patience*: The word must be pronounced
with three syllables.

266 *Impose me*: impose on me.
invention: The word here has only three
syllables (unlike the pronunciation at
line 276).

274 *Possess*: inform.

276 *invention*: imagination; the word here
has four syllables.
277–8 *Hang . . . tonight*: i.e. as suggested by
the friar, 4, 1, 205–7.

Almost the copy of my child that's dead,
And she alone is heir to both of us.
Give her the right you should have giv'n her cousin,
285 And so dies my revenge.

Claudio

O noble sir!
Your overkindness doth wring tears from me.
I do embrace your offer, and dispose
For henceforth of poor Claudio.

Leonato

Tomorrow then I will expect your coming;
290 Tonight I take my leave. This naughty man
Shall face to face be brought to Margaret,
Who, I believe, was pack'd in all this wrong,
Hir'd to it by your brother.

Borachio

No, by my soul, she was not;
Nor knew not what she did when she spoke to me,
295 But always hath been just and virtuous
In anything that I do know by her.

Dogberry

[*To* Leonato] Moreover, sir, which indeed is not
under white and black, this plaintiff here, the
offender, did call me ass. I beseech you let it be
300 remembered in his punishment. And also the watch
heard them talk of one Deformed. They say he wears
a key in his ear and lock hanging by it, and borrows
money in God's name, the which he hath used so
long and never paid, that now men grow hard-
305 hearted and will lend nothing for God's sake. Pray
you examine him upon that point.

Leonato

I thank thee for thy care and honest pains.

Dogberry

Your worship speaks like a most thankful and
reverend youth, and I praise God for you.

Leonato

310 [*Giving him money*] There's for thy pains.

Dogberry

God save the foundation!

Leonato

Go, I discharge thee of thy prisoner, and I thank
thee.

---

283 *heir . . . us*: Antonio's son (1, 2, 1) has been forgotten—and the daughter is an invention of the moment.

284 *right*: legal right *and* marriage rite.

290 *naughty*: wicked (the sense was stronger than it is today).

292 *pack'd*: involved as an accomplice.

298 *under . . . black*: written down.

301 *one Deformed*: 'what a deformed thief this fashion is' (3, 3, 115).

302 *a key . . . lock*: 'a wears a lock' (3, 3, 157–8); Dogberry elaborates the lovelock.

303 *in God's name*: a phrase commonly used by beggars: 'He that hath pity upon the poor lendeth unto the Lord' (Proverbs 19:17).
used: been in the habit of doing.

311 *God . . . foundation*: a phrase used by institutional beggars.

Dogberry

I leave an arrant knave with your worship, which I
315 beseech your worship to correct yourself, for the
example of others. God keep your worship; I wish
your worship well. God restore you to health. I
humbly give you leave to depart, and if a merry
meeting may be wished, God prohibit it. Come
320 neighbour.   [*Exeunt* Dogberry *and* Verges]

Leonato

Until tomorrow morning, lords, farewell.

Antonio

Farewell, my lords. We look for you tomorrow.

Don Pedro

We will not fail.

Claudio

Tonight I'll mourn with Hero.
                                   [*Exeunt* Don Pedro *and* Claudio]

Leonato

[*To the* Watch] Bring you these fellows on.—We'll
talk with Margaret,
325 How her acquaintance grew with this lewd fellow.
                                                            [*Exeunt*

325 *lewd*: base.

Act 5   Scene 2

Benedick tries to write a poem for Beatrice.

5 *so high a style*: Benedick puns on style
(= literary manner) and stile (= steps or
rungs for climbing over a fence); the
'high style' of literature was used only
for works of great seriousness.

6 *come over*: surpass, get across: Margaret
is quick to hear sexual innuendo.

9 *keep below stairs*: i.e. remain a servant
(and not become a mistress).

Scene 2

Enter Benedick *and* Margaret

Benedick

Pray thee, sweet Mistress Margaret, deserve well at
my hands by helping me to the speech of Beatrice.

Margaret

Will you then write me a sonnet in praise of my
beauty?

Benedick

5 In so high a style, Margaret, that no man living shall
come over it, for in most comely truth, thou
deservest it.

Margaret

To have no man come over me? Why, shall I always
keep below stairs?

11 *catches*: picks things up quickly.

15–16 *give . . . bucklers*: throw down my
defences ('bucklers' = small shields.

18–19 *put in . . . vice*: use a screw to fit the
pikes (into the bucklers).

24–7 *The god . . . deserve*: Benedick sings a
popular song—see 'Benedick's Song',
p.103.

28 *Leander*: In Greek mythology, Leander
swam every night across the Hellespont
that separated him from his beloved
Hero; the story is told in Christopher
Marlowe's poem *Hero and Leander*
(published 1598), which may have
suggested the name for Shakespeare's
character.

29 *Troilus*: In the Trojan War, Troilus was
introduced to Cressida by her uncle,
Pandarus; and their story is the subject
of Shakespeare's play *Troilus and
Cressida*.

30 *quondam carpet-mongers*: old-time ladies'
men (who frequented carpeted
boudoirs).

31 *yet*: still.

35 *innocent*: simple enough.

39 *festival terms*: flowery language.

Benedick

10 Thy wit is as quick as the greyhound's mouth; it
catches.   *Windhund*

Margaret

And yours as blunt as the fencer's foils, which hit but
hurt not.   *Fechters Folie*

Benedick

A most manly wit, Margaret; it will not hurt a

15 woman. And so, I pray thee, call Beatrice. I give thee
the bucklers.

Margaret

Give us the swords; we have bucklers of our own.

Benedick   *Beschützer*

If you use them, Margaret, you must put in the pikes
with a vice; and they are dangerous weapons for

20 maids.

Margaret

Well, I will call Beatrice to you, who I think hath
legs.   [*Exit*

Benedick

And therefore will come.

[*Sings*]

    The god of love

25   That sits above,

    And knows me, and knows me,

    How pitiful I deserve—

I mean in singing. But in loving—Leander the good
swimmer, Troilus the first employer of panders, and

30 a whole book full of these quondam carpet-mongers
whose names yet run smoothly in the even road of a
blank verse—why they were never so truly turned
over and over as my poor self in love. Marry, I
cannot show it in rhyme. I have tried. I can find out

35 no rhyme to 'lady' but 'baby'—an innocent rhyme;
for 'scorn' 'horn'—a hard rhyme; for 'school'
'fool'—a babbling rhyme. Very ominous endings.
No, I was not born under a rhyming planet, nor I
cannot woo in festival terms.

Enter Beatrice

40 Sweet Beatrice, wouldst thou come when I called
thee?

Beatrice

Yea, signor, and depart when you bid me.

Benedick

O, stay but till then.

Beatrice   *che*

'Then' is spoken. Fare you well now. And yet, ere I
45 go, let me go with that I came for, which is with
knowing what hath passed between you and Claudio.

Benedick

Only foul words, and thereupon I will kiss thee.

Beatrice

Foul words is but foul wind, and foul wind is but foul
49 *is noisome*: stinks.   breath, and foul breath is noisome. Therefore I will
50 depart unkissed.

Benedick

Thou hast frighted the word out of his right sense, so
forcible is thy wit. But I must tell thee plainly,
Claudio undergoes my challenge; and either I must
54 *subscribe him*: make a signed statement   shortly hear from him or I will subscribe him a
that he is.   55 coward. And I pray thee now tell me, for which of
my bad parts didst thou first fall in love with me?

Beatrice

For them all together, which maintained so politic a
57–8 *so . . . state*: such a well-organized   state of evil that they will not admit any good part to
rule.
vermischen intermingle with them. But for which of my good
60 parts did you first suffer love for me?

Benedick

61 *epithet*: expression.   'Suffer love'—a good epithet. I do suffer love indeed,
for I love thee against my will.

Beatrice

In spite of your heart, I think. Alas, poor heart! If
64 *spite it*: vex, irritate it.   you spite it for my sake I will spite it for yours, for I
65 will never love that which my friend hates.

Benedick

67 *appears not*: doesn't seem so.   Thou and I are too wise to woo peaceably.

Beatrice   *Geständnis*

It appears not in this confession. There's not one
wise man among twenty that will praise himself.

Benedick

An old, an old instance, Beatrice, that lived in the
70 time of good neighbours. If a man do not erect in
this age his own tomb ere he dies, he shall live no
longer in monument than the bell rings and the
widow weeps.

Beatrice

And how long is that, think you?

Benedick

75 Question—why, an hour in clamour and a quarter in
rheum. Therefore is it most expedient for the wise, if
Don Worm his conscience find no impediment to
the contrary, to be the trumpet of his own virtues, as
I am to myself. So much for praising myself who—I
80 myself will bear witness—is praiseworthy. And now
tell me, how doth your cousin?

Beatrice

Very ill.

Benedick

And how do you?

Beatrice

Very ill too.

Benedick

85 Serve God, love me, and mend. There will I leave
you too, for here comes one in haste.

Enter Ursula

Ursula

Madam, you must come to your uncle. Yonder's old
coil at home. It is proved my Lady Hero hath been
falsely accused, the prince and Claudio mightily
90 abused, and Don John is the author of all, who is fled
and gone. Will you come presently?

Beatrice

Will you go hear this news, signor?

Benedick

I will live in thy heart, die in thy lap, and be buried
in thy eyes; and, moreover, I will go with thee to thy
95 uncle's.   [*Exeunt*

69 *instance*: argument.
70 *good neighbours*: Benedick alludes to a proverb: 'He who praises himself has ill neighbours'.
72 *in monument*: in remembrance.

75 *Question*: good question—and Benedick provides the answer.
76 *rheum*: tears.
77 *Don Worm*: The worm, gnawing inwardly, is a traditional image for the conscience (Isaiah 66:24, Mark 9:44).

87–8 *old coil*: great confusion, much ado.

90 *abused*: deceived.
91 *presently*: immediately.

93 *die*: Benedick's romanticism includes the word's sexual sense (= orgasm).

Claudio performs his duties at Hero's tomb.

os.d. *tapers*: wax candles for devotional
use.

5 *guerdon of*: recompense for.

Scene 3

Enter Claudio, Don Pedro *the prince, and
three or four* Attendants *with tapers, all
wearing mourning*; Balthasar *and*
musicians

Claudio
Is this the monument of Leonato?
A Lord
It is, my lord.
Claudio
[*Reading from a scroll*]
   Done to death by slanderous tongues
     Was the Hero that here lies.
5   Death, in guerdon of her wrongs,
     Gives her fame which never dies.
   So the life that died with shame
   Lives in death with glorious fame.

     He hangs the epitaph on the tomb

   Hang thou there upon the tomb,
10   Praising her when I am dumb.
Now music sound, and sing your solemn hymn.

     Musicians play

11 **Balthasar**: The singer of *Act 2, Scene 3*. No singer is named in the Quarto text, although lines 12–21 are marked 'Song'.

12 *goddess of the night*: Diana, the moon-goddess, protector of virgins (her 'knights').

15 *Round . . . go*: The mourners circle the tomb clockwise in a propitiatory dance.

20 *uttered*: utterèd; expressed, set forth; the rhyme here is more important than the sense.

24–33 *Good morrow . . . woe*: The rhyming lines declare the closure of an episode.

26 *wheels of Phoebus*: chariot of the sun-god.

29 *several*: separate.

30 *weeds*: garments.

32 *Hymen*: god of marriage.
luckier issue: more fortunate outcome.
speeds: hastens.

Balthasar
[*Sings*]
  Pardon, goddess of the night,
  Those that slew thy virgin knight, Ritter
  For the which with songs of woe Jammer, Weh
15 Round about her tomb they go.
    Midnight, assist our moan,
    Help us to sigh and groan,   säufzen
      Heavily, heavily.
  Graves yawn, and yield your dead
20 Till death be uttered,
    Heavily, heavily.
  Claudio
  Now, unto thy bones good night.
  Yearly will I do this rite.
  Don Pedro
Good morrow, masters, put your torches out.
25   The wolves have prey'd, and look, the gentle day
Before the wheels of Phoebus round about
  Dapples the drowsy east with spots of grey.
Thanks to you all, and leave us. Fare you well.
  Claudio
Good morrow, masters. Each his several way.
  Don Pedro sein lassen
30 Come, let us hence, and put on other weeds, Unkraut
And then to Leonato's we will go.
  Claudio
And Hymen now with luckier issue speeds
Than this for whom we render'd up this woe.
              [*Exeunt*

Act 5   Scene 4

Claudio, prepared to meet his new bride, is reunited with Hero, then Benedick joins hands with Beatrice and leads the company off into a final dance.

6 *question*: investigation.

7 *sorts*: turns out.

8 *faith*: honour.

14 *office*: function.

17 *confirm'd countenance*: a straight face; 'confirm'd' must be stressed on the first syllable.

20 *undo me*: ruin me, release me (from the pose of misogynist).

Scene 4

Enter Leonato, Antonio, Benedick,
Beatrice, Margaret, Ursula, Friar Francis,
and Hero

Friar
Did I not tell you she was innocent?
Leonato
So are the prince and Claudio, who accus'd her
Upon the error that you heard debated.
But Margaret was in some fault for this,
5 Although against her will, as it appears
In the true course of the question.
Antonio
Well, I am glad that all things sorts so well.
Benedick
And so am I, being else by faith enforc'd
To call young Claudio to a reckoning for it.
Leonato
10 Well, daughter, and you gentlewomen all,
Withdraw into a chamber by yourselves,
And when I send for you, come hither mask'd.
        [*Exeunt* Beatrice, Hero, Margaret, *and* Ursula
The prince and Claudio promis'd by this hour
To visit me. [*To* Antonio] You know your office,
    brother;
15 You must be father to your brother's daughter,
And give her to young Claudio.
Antonio
Which I will do with confirm'd countenance.
Benedick
Friar, I must entreat your pains, I think.
Friar
To do what, signor?
Benedick
20 To bind me or undo me, one of them.
Signor Leonato, truth it is, good signor,
Your niece regards me with an eye of favour.
Leonato
That eye my daughter lent her, 'tis most true.
Benedick
And I do with an eye of love requite her.

Leonato

25 The sight whereof I think you had from me,
From Claudio and the prince. But what's your will?

Benedick

Your answer, sir, is enigmatical. rätselhaft
But for my will—my will is your good will
May stand with ours this day to be conjoin'd
30 In the state of honourable marriage—
In which, good friar, I shall desire your help.

Leonato

My heart is with your liking.

Friar

                              And my help.
Here comes the prince and Claudio.

Enter Don Pedro *and* Claudio *with*
Attendants

Don Pedro

Good morrow to this fair assembly.

Leonato

35 Good morrow, Prince. Good morrow, Claudio.
We here attend you. Are you yet determin'd entschlossen
Today to marry with my brother's daughter?

Claudio

I'll hold my mind, were she an Ethiope.

Leonato

Call her forth, brother; here's the friar ready.

[*Exit* Antonio

Don Pedro

40 Good morrow, Benedick. Why, what's the matter
That you have such a February face,
So full of frost, of storm and cloudiness?

Claudio

I think he thinks upon the savage bull.
Tush, fear not, man, we'll tip thy horns with gold,
45 And all Europa shall rejoice at thee
As once Europa did at lusty Jove
When he would play the noble beast in love.

Benedick   liebenswürdig

Bull Jove, sir, had an amiable low,   Tief
And some such strange bull leapt your father's cow
50 And got a calf in that same noble feat
Much like to you, for you have just his bleat.

30 *marriage*: The word must be
pronounced with three syllables.

34 *assembly*: This word needs four syllables
for regularity.

38 *Ethiope*: Ethiopian—i.e. very dark
(suntan was most unfashionable at this
time).

41 *February face*: Benedick still shows his
disapproval of Don Pedro and Claudio.

43–7 *savage bull . . . love*: Classical
mythology tells how Jupiter (Jove)
transformed himself into a bull and
carried off the princess Europa.

44 *tip . . . gold*: make you a glorious
cuckold.

45 *all Europa*: i.e. the entire continent of
Europe.

46 *once Europa did*: i.e. the princess Europa.

Enter Antonio *with* Hero, Beatrice,
Margaret, *and* Ursula, *the ladies masked*

Claudio
For this I owe you. Here comes other reck'nings.
Which is the lady I must seize upon?

Antonio   nehmen, fassen
This same is she, and I do give you her.

Claudio
55 Why then, she's mine. Sweet, let me see your face.

Leonato
No, that you shall not till you take her hand
Before this friar and swear to marry her.

Claudio
[*To* Hero] Give me your hand before this holy friar.
I am your husband, if you like of me.

Hero
60 [*Unmasking*] And when I liv'd I was your other wife;
And when you lov'd, you were my other husband.

Claudio
Another Hero!

Hero
                Nothing certainer.
One Hero died defil'd, but I do live,
And surely as I live, I am a maid.

Don Pedro
65 The former Hero, Hero that is dead!

Leonato
She died, my lord, but whiles her slander liv'd.

Friar
All this amazement can I qualify.
When after that the holy rites are ended
I'll tell you largely of fair Hero's death.
70 Meantime let wonder seem familiar,
And to the chapel let us presently.

Benedick
Soft and fair, friar; which is Beatrice?

Beatrice
[*Unmasking*] I answer to that name. What is your
will?

Benedick
Do not you love me?

67 *qualify*: moderate.

69 *largely*: fully.

71 *presently*: at once.

72 *Soft and fair*: take it easy.

Beatrice

              Why no, no more than reason.

Benedick

75 Why then, your uncle and the prince and Claudio

Have been deceiv'd. They swore you did.

Beatrice

Do not you love me?

Benedick

              Troth no, no more than reason.

Beatrice

Why then, my cousin, Margaret, and Ursula

Are much deceiv'd, for they did swear you did.

Benedick

80 They swore that you were almost sick for me.

Beatrice

They swore that you were well nigh dead for me.

Benedick

'Tis no such matter. Then you do not love me?

Beatrice

No, truly, but in friendly recompense.

Leonato

Come, cousin, I am sure you love the gentleman.

Claudio

85 And I'll be sworn upon't that he loves her,

For here's a paper written in his hand,

A halting sonnet of his own pure brain,

Fashion'd to Beatrice.

Hero

             And here's another,

Writ in my cousin's hand, stol'n from her pocket,

90 Containing her affection unto Benedick.

Benedick

A miracle! Here's our own hands against our hearts.

Come, I will have thee. But by this light, I take thee

for pity.

Beatrice

I would not deny you. But by this good day, I yield

95 upon great persuasion, and partly to save your life,

for I was told you were in a consumption.

Benedick

[*Kissing her*] Peace, I will stop your mouth.

Don Pedro

How dost thou, 'Benedick the married man'?

83 *but in . . . recompense*: except as a return of friendship.

87 *halting*: metrically lame.

101 *satire . . . epigram*: These forms of
     ridicule were popular at the time.
102 *wear nothing handsome*: not wear
     fashionable clothes (which were an easy
     and popular target for satirists).
105 *flout*: mock.
106 *giddy*: inconstant.

113 *double dealer*: i.e. an unfaithful husband.

122–3 *There . . . horn*: The play's final
       allusion to the horns of the cuckold; the
       'staff' is 'reverend' because it is a
       symbol of authority, and old age.
126 *brave*: fine.

Benedick
I'll tell thee what, Prince: a college of wit-crackers
100 cannot flout me out of my humour. Dost thou think
I care for a satire or an epigram? No, if a man will be
beaten with brains, a shall wear nothing handsome
about him. In brief, since I do purpose to marry, I
will think nothing to any purpose that the world can
105 say against it. And therefore never flout at me for
what I have said against it. For man is a giddy thing,
and this is my conclusion. For thy part, Claudio, I
did think to have beaten thee, but in that thou art
like to be my kinsman, live unbruised, and love my
110 cousin.

Claudio
I had well hoped thou wouldst have denied Beatrice,
that I might have cudgelled thee out of thy single life
to make thee a double dealer, which out of question
thou wilt be, if my cousin do not look exceeding
115 narrowly to thee.

Benedick
Come, come, we are friends. Let's have a dance ere
we are married, that we may lighten our own hearts
and our wives' heels.

Leonato
We'll have dancing afterward.

Benedick
120 First, of my word! Therefore play, music. [*To* Don
Pedro] Prince, thou art sad. Get thee a wife, get thee
a wife. There is no staff more reverend than one
tipped with horn.

Enter Messenger

Messenger
My lord, your brother John is ta'en in flight,
125 And brought with armed men back to Messina.

Benedick
Think not on him till tomorrow. I'll devise thee brave
punishments for him. Strike up, pipers.

[*Dance, and exeunt*

Benedick's Song

High in the charts in the sixteenth century was the song that Benedick attempts to sing when he is waiting for Beatrice in Act v, Scene ii. Its author was William Elderton, actor, singer, and songwriter, who died in about 1592. The song's popularity is vouched for by the number of imitations, parodies, and references in the literature of the period. It was set to a well-known dance tune called 'Turkeyloney'.

1   The gods of love that sits about
      and know me, and know me,
         how sorrowful I do serve,
  grant my request that at the least,
    she show me, she show me,
      some pity when I deserve;
  that every brawl may turn to bliss,
    to joy with all that joyful is.
      Do this my dear and bind me
  for ever and ever your own;
    And as you here do find me
      so let your love be shown,
  for till I hear this unity
    I languish in extremity.

2   As yet I have a soul to save
    uprightly, uprightly;
      though troubled with despair,
  I cannot find to set my mind
    so lightly, so slightly,
      as die before you be there.
  But since I must needs you provoke,
    come slake the thirst, stand by the stroke,
  that when my heart is fainted
    the sorrowful sighs may tell
  you might have been acquainted
    with one that loved you well.
  None have I told the jeopardy
    that none but you can remedy . . .

5   With courtesy now so bend, so bow,
      to speed me, to speed me,
         as answereth my desire;
     as I will be if ever I see
       you need, you need me,
         as ready when you require.
     Unworthy though to come so nigh
       that passing show that feeds mine eye,
     yet shall I die without it
       if pity be not in you.
        But sure I do not doubt it
    nor anything you can do –
    to whom I do commit, and shall,
       my self to work your will with all.

       finis

'A Hero-ic puzzle'

The author of *Alice in Wonderland*, Lewis Carroll, was quick to appreciate the many improbabilities in the plot of *Much Ado About Nothing*. He amused himself by pointing out some of them to Ellen Terry, a famous actress of the time.

Christ Church
Oxford
20 March 1883

Dear Mrs Wardell [Ellen Terry's married name],

I'm going to put before you a 'Hero-ic' puzzle of mine –

Why in the world did not Hero (or at any rate Beatrice speaking on her behalf) prove an 'alibi', in answer to the charge? It seems certain she did *not* sleep in her own room that night: for how could Margaret venture to open the window and talk from it, with her mistress asleep in the room? It would be sure to wake her. Besides, Borachio says, after promising that Margaret shall speak with him out of Hero's chamber-window, 'I will so fashion the matter that Hero shall be absent'. (How *he* could possibly manage any such thing is another difficulty: but I pass over that.)

Well then, granting that Hero slept in some other room that night why didn't she say so? When Claudio asks her, 'What man was he talked with you yesternight Out at your window betwixt twelve and one?' why doesn't she reply, 'I talked with no man at that hour, my lord: Nor was I in my chamber yesternight, But in another, far from it remote'. And this she could of course prove by the evidence of the housemaid, who *must* have known that she had occupied another room that night.

But even if *Hero* might be supposed to be so distracted as not to remember where she had slept the night before, or even whether she had slept *anywhere*, surely *Beatrice* has her wits about her? And when an arrangement was made, by which she was to lose, for that one night, her twelve-months' bedfellow, is it conceivable that she didn't know *where* Hero passed the night? Why didn't she reply

> But, good my lord, sweet Hero slept not there:
> She had another chamber for the nonce.
> 'Twas sure some counterfeit that did present
> Her person at the window, aped her voice,

Her mien, her manners, and hath thus deceived
My good lord Pedro and this company?

With all these excellent materials for proving an 'alibi', it is incomprehensible that no one should think of it. If only there had been a barrister present, to cross-examine Beatrice! 'Now, ma'am, attend to me, if you please: and speak up, so that the jury may hear you. Where did you sleep last night? Where did Hero sleep? Will you swear that she slept in her own room? Will you swear you do not know where she slept? Etc, etc' . . .

C. L. Dodgson (Lewis Carroll)

From *The Letters of Lewis Carroll*, ed. Morton N. Cohen (1979), i. 488.

Background

England in 1599

When Shakespeare was writing *Much Ado About Nothing*, many people still believed that the sun went round the earth. They were taught that this was the way God had ordered things, and that – in England – God had founded a Church and appointed a Monarchy so that the land and people could be well governed.

'The past is a foreign country; they do things differently there.'

L. P. Hartley

Government

For most of Shakespeare's life, the reigning monarch of England was Queen Elizabeth I. With her counsellors and ministers, she governed the nation from London, although fewer than half a million people out of a total population of six million lived in the capital city. In the rest of the country, law and order were maintained by the land-owners and enforced by their deputies. The average man had no vote, and women had no rights at all.

Religion

At this time, England was a Christian country. All children were baptized, soon after they were born, into the Church of England; they were taught the essentials of the Christian faith, and instructed in their duty to God and to humankind. Marriages and funerals were conducted only by the licensed clergy and according to the Church's rites and ceremonies. Attending divine service was compulsory; absences (without a good medical reason) could be punished by fines. By such means, the authorities were able to keep some control over the population – recording births, marriages, and deaths; being alert to anyone who refused to accept standard religious practices, who could be politically dangerous; and ensuring that people received the approved teachings through the official 'Homilies' which were regularly preached in all parish churches.

Elizabeth I's father, Henry VIII, had broken away from the Church of Rome, and from that time all people in England were able to hear the church services *in their own language* rather than in Latin. The Book of Common Prayer was used in every church, and an English translation of the Bible was read aloud in public. The Christian religion had never been so well taught before!

Education

School education reinforced the Church's teaching. From the age of four, boys might attend the 'petty school' (its name came from the French '*petite école*') to learn reading and writing along with a few prayers; some schools also included work with numbers. At the age of seven, the boy was ready for the grammar school (if his father was willing and able to pay the fees).

Grammar schools taught Latin grammar, translation work and the study of Roman authors, paying attention as much to style as to content. The art of fine writing was therefore important from early youth. A very few students went on to university; these were either clever boys who won scholarships, or else the sons of rich noblemen. Girls stayed at home, and learned domestic and social skills – cooking, sewing, perhaps even music. The lucky ones might learn to read and write.

Language

At the start of the sixteenth century the English had a very poor opinion of their own language: there was little serious writing in English, and hardly any literature. Latin was the language of international scholarship, and the eloquent style of the Romans was much admired. Many translations from Latin were made, and in this way writers increased the vocabulary of English and made its grammar more flexible. French, Italian, and Spanish works were also translated and, for the first time, there were English versions of the Bible. By the end of the century, English was a language to be proud of: it was rich in vocabulary, capable of infinite variety and subtlety, and ready for all kinds of word-play – especially *puns*, for which Elizabethan English is renowned.

Drama

The great art-form of the Elizabethan and Jacobean age was its drama. The Elizabethans inherited a tradition of play-acting from the Middle Ages, and they reinforced this by reading and translating the Roman playwrights. At the beginning of the sixteenth century plays were performed by groups of actors. These were all-male companies (boys acted the female roles) who travelled from town to town, setting up their stages in open places (such as inn-yards) or, with the permission of the owner, in the hall of some noble house. The touring companies continued outside London into the seventeenth century; but in London, in 1576, a new building was erected for the performance of plays. This was the Theatre, the first purpose-built playhouse in England. Other playhouses followed, including the Globe, where most of Shakespeare's plays were performed, and English drama reached new heights.

There were people who disapproved, of course. The theatres, which brought large crowds together, could encourage the spread of disease – and dangerous ideas. During the summer, when the plague was at its worst, the playhouses were closed. A constant censorship was imposed, more or less severe at different times. The Puritans, a religious and political faction who wanted to impose strict rules of behaviour, tried to close down the theatres. However, partly because the royal family favoured drama, and partly because the buildings were outside the city limits, they did not succeed until 1642.

Theatre

From contemporary comments and sketches – most particularly a drawing by a Dutch visitor, Johannes de Witt – it is possible to form some idea of the typical Elizabethan playhouse for which most of Shakespeare's plays were written. Hexagonal (six-sided) in shape, it had three roofed galleries encircling an open courtyard. The plain, high stage projected into the yard, where it was surrounded by the audience of standing 'groundlings'. At the back were two doors for the actors' entrances and exits; and above these doors was a balcony – useful for a musicians' gallery or for the acting of scenes '*above*'. Over the stage was a thatched roof, supported on two pillars, forming a canopy – which seems to have been painted with the sun, moon, and stars for the 'heavens'.

Underneath was space (concealed by curtains) which could b[e] used by characters ascending and descending through a trap-doo[r] in the stage. Costumes and properties were kept backstage in th[e] 'tiring house'. The actors used the most luxurious costumes the[y] could find, often clothes given to them by rich patrons. Stag[e] properties were important for showing where a scene was set, bu[t] the dramatist's own words were needed to explain the time of day[,] since all performances took place in the early afternoon.

A replica of Shakespeare's own theatre, the Globe, has bee[n] built in London, and stands in Southwark, almost exactly on th[e] Bankside site of the original.

William Shakespeare, 1564–1616

Elizabeth I was Queen of England when Shakespeare was born in 1564. He was the son of a tradesman who made and sold gloves in the small town of Stratford-upon-Avon, and he was educated at the grammar school in that town. Shakespeare did not go to university when he left school, but worked, perhaps, in his father's business. When he was eighteen he married Anne Hathaway, who became the mother of his daughter, Susanna, in 1583, and of twins in 1585.

There is nothing exciting, or even unusual, in this story; and from 1585 until 1592 there are no documents that can tell us anything at all about Shakespeare. But we have learned that in 1592 he was known in London, and that he had become both an actor and a playwright.

We do not know when Shakespeare wrote his first play, and we are not sure of the order in which he wrote his works. If you look on page 113 at the list of his writings and their approximate dates, you will see he started by writing plays on subjects taken from the history of England. No doubt this was partly because he was patriotic and interested in English history, but he was also a very shrewd businessman. He could see that the theatre audiences enjoyed being shown their own history, and it was certain that he would make a profit from this kind of drama.

He also wrote comedies, with romantic love-stories of young people who fall in love with one another, and at the end of the play marry and live happily ever after.

At the end of the sixteenth century Shakespeare wrote some melancholy, bitter, and tragic plays. This change may have been caused by some sadness in the writer's life (his only son died in 1596). Shakespeare, however, was not the only writer whose works at this time were very serious. The whole of England was facing a crisis. Queen Elizabeth I was growing old. She was greatly loved, and the people were sad to think she must soon die; they were also afraid, because the queen had never married, and so there was no child to succeed her.

When James I, Elizabeth's Scottish cousin, came to the thron
in 1603, Shakespeare continued to write serious drama – the grea
tragedies and the plays based on Roman history (such as *Juli*
Caesar) for which he is most famous. Finally, before he retired from
the theatre, he wrote another set of comedies. These all have th
same theme: they tell of happiness which is lost, and then foun
again.

Shakespeare returned from London to Stratford, his hom
town. He was rich and successful, and he owned one of the bigges
houses in the town. He died in 1616.

Shakespeare also wrote two long poems, and a collection c
sonnets. The sonnets describe two love affairs, but we do nc
know who the lovers were – or whether they existed only i
Shakespeare's imagination. Although there are many publi
documents concerned with his career as a writer and
businessman, Shakespeare has hidden his personal life from us.
nineteenth-century poet, Matthew Arnold, addressed Shakespear
in a poem, and wrote 'We ask and ask – Thou smilest, and ar
still'.

Approximate Dates of Composition of Shakespeare's Works

Period	Comedies	History plays	Tragedies	Poems
I before 1594	Comedy of Errors Taming of the Shrew Two Gentlemen of Verona Love's Labour's Lost	Henry VI, part 1 Henry VI, part 2 Henry VI, part 3 Richard III	Titus Andronicus	Venus and Adonis Rape of Lucrece
II 1594 – 1599	Midsummer Night's Dream Merchant of Venice Merry Wives of Windsor Much Ado About Nothing As You Like It	Richard II King John Henry IV, part 1 Henry IV, part 2 Henry V	Romeo and Juliet	Sonnets
III 1599 – 1608	Twelfth Night Troilus and Cressida Measure for Measure All's Well That Ends Well Pericles		Julius Caesar Hamlet Othello Timon of Athens King Lear Macbeth Antony and Cleopatra Coriolanus	
IV 1608 – 1613	Cymbeline The Winter's Tale The Tempest	Henry VIII		

Exploring Much Ado About Nothing in the Classroom

Shakespeare's comedies abound with exaggerated characters and scenarios, witty and sharp dialogue, humorous misunderstandings, bawdiness, puns, parodies and malapropisms – and *Much Ado About Nothing* is no exception. There are layers of humour in the play waiting to be explored by students of different ages.

This section suggests a range of approaches in the classroom, to engender both enjoyment and understanding of the play.

Ways into the Play

Students may feel an antipathy towards the study of Shakespeare. The imaginative and enthusiastic teacher, with the help of this edition of the play, will soon break this down!

Navigating the play

If this is the first time your students have looked at a whole Shakespeare play, or at this particular edition, give them some practice at finding their way around. After explaining the division into acts, scenes and lines, challenge them to look up some references as quickly as possible. (They can also test each other with their own references.) Below are some suggestions that might lead on to further discussion of the themes and the plot.

Act I, Scene i, lines 171–2   (*In mine eye she is the sweetest lady that ever I looked on.*)

Act I, Scene iii, lines 27–8   (*…it must not be denied but I am a plain-dealing villain.*)

Act II, Scene i, lines 16–17   (*…thou wilt never get thee a husband if thou be so shrewd of thy tongue.*)

Improvisation

Give students a choice of the following modern scenarios to act out.

a)   One person really likes another. His/her friend tries to act as a 'go-between' and arrange a date.

b)   A piece of nasty gossip incriminates one person in a group of friends. How do the others react?

c)   Two old acquaintances – Ben and Bea – seem not to get along, but the rest of their friends try to engineer a date. They tell a few white lies. What happens?

Setting the Scene

A comedy

Much Ado About Nothing is a comedy mainly about love. Ask your students what sort of situations and characters they will expect to find in such a play. This comedy also has some serious and unhappy moments, so discuss why such scenes are included. Is the same mix of comic and serious to be found in modern film or television comedies?

Old and new

The issues at the heart of the play – love and marriage – will be familiar to your students, as should the ideas of dishonesty, deception and mischief, but the presentation of these ideas and issues have an Elizabethan context that will need some explanation. You may need to help bridge the divide of 400 years since the play was written by giving more information on:

- the importance of honour
- the lack of power accorded to women in their own right
- parent and daughter relationships
- the situation of those born out of wedlock (Don John).

Students will also benefit from some exploration of the conventions of Elizabethan theatre. Devise a 'true or false' quiz or card sort, using statements such as:

- All the parts were played by men or boys. (True)
- The plays were only performed in the evening. (False)
- They used very little scenery. (True)
- Only the rich went to the plays. (False)

Discuss the effects of these conventions on the performance of the play.

Keeping Track of the Action

It's important to give students opportunities to 'digest' and reflect upon their reading, so that they may take ownership of the play.

Reading journal

As you read through the play, help your students to trace and understand the plot by asking them to keep a journal in which they record what happens, as well as their reactions and thoughts about the action and the characters. Their responses can remain focused through specific questions (from the teacher) to answer. As part of their journal they can keep a timeline of the main events, or a lovers' timeline which charts the developments between Claudio and Hero, and Benedick and Beatrice.

Storyboarding

Cartoon strip versions of scenes can be helpful for younger students in particular. Give them an example of how to sum up the action, in pictures, captions (explaining what is happening) and speech/thought bubbles (for key words and lines), and then ask them to complete their own storyboard. Suitable scenes might be:

- Act II, Scene i, lines 77–195 – have each 'frame' showing a different conversation at the masked ball
- Act II, Scene iii, lines 92–252: part one of Don Pedro's scheme to make Benedick and Beatrice fall in love
- Act III, Scene i: part two of Don Pedro's scheme to make Benedick and Beatrice fall in love.

Film versions

Using a film of the play, such as the Kenneth Branagh version, is a helpful and illuminating way of making the play accessible to students. Exploring different interpretations and treatments can give real insight. Students may be able to develop this into a piece of coursework that examines a director's interpretation of the play.

Sequencing and Cloze

You can test your students' grasp of key parts of the action by summarizing the plot in a number of sentences, jumbling the sentences and asking students to place them in the correct sequence. Alternatively, give a modern English summary of a scene studied, leaving key words/characters' names blank, and ask students to complete the blanks.

Characters

Students of all ages need to come to an understanding of the characters: their motivations, their relationships and their development.

Casting director

Ask your students to cast the parts for a new film or stage version of *Much Ado About Nothing*. First, they will need to construct a profile on the characters containing information about them (known and surmised). Next, they must make a report on which actors they are going to invite to take the parts, and why. Finally, they should give each actor important information about their character, and suggestions on how to play the part.

Character development

Shakespeare's characters are multi-faceted – they make mistakes, change their minds and learn life's lessons, just like the rest of us. Ask your students to analyse the development of one character, Benedick, for example. Look at how Benedick's attitude to love and to Beatrice changes over the course of three speeches (Act II, Scene i, lines 221–42; Act II, Scene iii, lines 3–36; Act II, Scene iii, lines 210–35). Ask them to describe, explain and evaluate the changes experienced by Benedick.

Diaries, letters and reports

Giving your students the opportunity to write and think as one of the characters provides them with a new and illuminating perspective on the character(s). Here are some possible scenarios:

a)   Claudio experiences a whole range of emotions during the play: first love, betrayal (as he thinks), guilt. Create a range of diary entries which look at the issues from Claudio's viewpoint, and which reveal his feelings and reactions.

b)   Don John is embittered about his illegitimacy and his situation. Ask students to compose a letter his brother, Don Pedro, expressing his frustrations and the reasons for his actions in the play.

c)   Explain the purpose of an obituary to your students. Ask them to imagine that Beatrice writes an obituary for Hero after her supposed death. Remembering that Beatrice believes completely in Hero's innocence, what will she write?

Themes

Love, honour and deception are all themes that can be easily explored in this play.

The language of love

Don Pedro jokes with Claudio that he will 'tire the hearer with a book of words'. Ask your students to pick out Claudio's words of love from Act I, Scene i and to discuss the 'proper' and rather polished language he uses. They can then use the words to compose Claudio's book of words (or poetry) about love.

Masks and deceptions

Ask your students to list all the deceptions that take place in the play, both malevolent and benign, and discuss the dramatic purposes and impact of the deceptions. Ask them to design a mask for one of the characters to wear in the masked ball in Act II, Scene i. The mask must say something about the character's personality or role in the play, and may be derived from lines of the play.

Love, honour and obey...

There are very clear ideas of correct female behaviour. Look at the scene where Hero is accused of infidelity and unchaste behaviour. Pick out the language that shows the seriousness and outrage behind the accusations. Hero seems quite helpless in this scene. Who stands up for her? Discuss the different expectations on men and women, and how they were expected to maintain their honour. More able students could discuss Shakespeare's probable intentions in his portrayal of Hero and Claudio – is there any message behind the situation?

Shakespeare's Language

The language of *Much Ado About Nothing* is particularly rich in images, rhetoric and sharp wit.

Imagery

Invite your students to search for striking imagery relating to people. Beatrice, for example, is described as 'a rare parrot-teacher', Benedick as having a 'February face' and Hero as a 'rotten orange'. Ask your students to choose a character (Benedick and Beatrice are the easiest), to draw a picture of the character and surround the picture with some of the images they've found in the words of the play. If this is done on OHT, students can share their ideas with the class, and they can use a second OHT to build a layer of explanation onto the images.

Prose and verse

Unusually, *Much Ado About Nothing* is written mainly in prose, as opposed to blank verse. Scanning through the play should tell your students that the verse is mainly reserved for the romance and dramatic scenes between Hero and Claudio. Discuss the effect this has, and challenge your students to write their own verse in iambic pentameter – perhaps a rhyming couplet – summing up the story of Hero and Claudio.

In a word

Shakespeare was a clever wordsmith who enjoyed playing with words. He frequently extracts more than one meaning from a word, and will use the same word in a number of ways in the same breath, for example 'Balthasar: *Note this before my notes: There's not a note of mine that worth noting*'. Indeed, in Shakespeare's day the word 'nothing' would have been pronounced as 'noting' which adds an extra dimension to the title. Discuss the implications this has for the meaning of the play's title. Encourage your students to keep their own notes – perhaps in their reading journal – noting down words and phrases of interest and significance.

Exploring with Drama

Book the hall or push back the desks, because the best way to study a great play is through drama. Students of all ages will benefit from a dramatic encounter with *Much Ado About Nothing*. They will enjoy the opportunity to act out a scene or two, or to explore the scenes through improvisation, for example, putting a character in the 'hot seat' for questioning by others.

Tableaux

Ask your students to create a tableau, in groups, which contains all the main characters from the play. The positions of the characters should say something about their relationships and position within the play. Bring the tableaux briefly to life by having each person saying something in character.

Playing the fool

Dogberry and Verges are comic characters who unwittingly bring about the resolution of the play. Challenge your students to act out a modern language version of Act IV, Scene ii where they examine the prisoners, but maintaining the misunderstandings and malapropisms.

A performance

Students will enjoy the opportunity to act out a significant scene from the play. Let them choose a director who will interpret and lead the performance. This speaking and listening work can be followed up with an evaluation of the scene, Shakespeare's probable intentions, and their own interpretation and performance.

Writing about *Much Ado About Nothing*

If your students have to write about the play for coursework or for examinations, you may wish to give them this general guidance:

- Read the question or task carefully, highlight the key words and answer all parts of the question.
- Planning is essential. Plan what will be in each paragraph.
- You can change your plan if necessary.
- Avoid retelling the story.
- *Much Ado About Nothing* is a play – so be ready to consider the impact or effect on the audience.
- Use the Point, Evidence, Explanation (PEE) structure to explain points.
- Adding Evaluation (PEEE!) will gain you higher marks.
- Keep quotations short and relevant.
- Avoid referring to a film version of the play, unless this is part of your task.

Further Reading and Resources

General

Fantasia, Louis, *Instant Shakespeare: a practical guide for actors, directors and teachers* (A & C Black, 2002).

Greer, Germaine, *Shakespeare A Very Short Introduction* (Oxford, 2002).

Hall, Peter, *Shakespeare's Advice to the Players* (Oberon Books, 2003).

Holden, Anthony, *Shakespeare: his life and work* (Abacus, 2002).

McConnell, Louise, *Exit, pursued by a bear – Shakespeare's characters, plays, poems, history and stagecraft* (Bloomsbury, 2003).

McLeish and Unwin, *A Pocket Guide to Shakespeare's Plays* (Faber and Faber, 1998).

Wood, Michael, *In Search of Shakespeare* (BBC, 2003).

Children's/Students' books

Carpenter, Humphrey, *More Shakespeare Without the Boring Bits* (Viking, 1997).

Ganeri, Anita, *What they don't tell you about Shakespeare* (Hodder, 1996).

Williams, Marcia, *Bravo, Mr William Shakespeare!* (Walker, 2001).

Websites

Elizabethan pronunciation
Including information on insults.
http://www.renfaire.com/Language/index.html

Encyclopaedia Britannica – Shakespeare and the Globe: Then and Now
Information about the Globe and the theatre in Shakespeare's times.
http://search.eb.com/shakespeare/index2.html

The Royal Shakespeare Company website
As well as information on the theatre company, there are
resources on the plays and the life and times of Shakespeare.
http://www.rsc.org.uk/home/index.asp

The Shakespeare Birthplace Trust
Information on his works, life and times.
http://www.shakespeare.org.uk/homepage

Shakespeare's Globe
Information on the Globe Theatre, London.
http://www.shakespeares-globe.org/

Shakespeare High
A Shakespeare classroom on the Internet.
http://www.shakespearehigh.com/

Spark Notes: Much Ado About Nothing
An online study guide.
http://www.sparknotes.com/shakespeare/muchado/

Mr William Shakespeare and the Internet
A comprehensive guide to Shakespeare resources on the Internet.
http://shakespeare.palomar.edu/

Film, video and DVD

Much Ado About Nothing
Directed by Kenneth Branagh (1993)
Starring Kenneth Branagh, Emma Thompson

Much Ado About Nothing
BBC Shakespeare Collection